F*ck You I'm Irish

Why We Irish Are Awesome

Rashers Tierney

Ulysses Press

Published by:
Ulysses Press
P.O. Box 3440
Berkeley, CA 94703
www.ulyssespress.com

ISBN: 978-1-61243-406-3
Library of Congress Control Number: 2014943020

Printed in the United States by Bang Printing

10 9 8 7 6 5 4 3 2 1

Acquisitions Editor: Katherine Furman
Project Manager: Kelly Reed
Managing Editor: Claire Chun
Editor: Renee Rutledge
Proofreader: Lauren Harrison
Production: Jake Flaherty
Cover design: what!design @ whatweb.com
Cover images: from shutterstock.com – clover © serazetdinov;
    beer © borsvelka; background texture © secondcorner;
    harp © Pim; border © RedKoala
Interior images: from shutterstock.com – chapter graphic
    © tanik; section and folio graphics © RAEVSKY; map ©
    JBOY

Distributed by Publishers Group West

Contents

1. Setting Aside the Clichés. 5

2. How the Irish Made America 14

3. Hope and Heavy Hearts 38

4. Bloody Ingenious 50

5. From Guinness to Whisk-e-y 64

6. Irish Pop Culture and Its
   Worldwide Impact 78

7. Ireland's Legacy of Learning
   and Knowledge 95

8. A Way with Words Like You
   Wouldn't Believe. 106

9. More Magic and Mystery Than
   You Could Shake a Stick At. 130

10. Religion. 144

11. Irish Bad-Asses 156

12. Sexy and Romantic Sons of Bitches 167

13. Hell of a History in the Homeland 176

14. Gaelic Geography Lesson. 184

About the Author. 192

CHAPTER 1

Setting Aside the Clichés

From our fightin' nature and inherent good luck to our potato eating and St. Patrick's Day parading, the clichés regarding us Irish are famous. But our true awesomeness stems not from a few lame stereotypes; rather it can be found in the countless accomplishments for which we're not given proper credit. That is— until now! Serving up the truth like a perfect pint of Guinness, here are the fun and informative facts about the best feckin' people in the world—the Irish. Astonishing historical accounts. Profiles of Irish heroes. Stories of struggles and success. Language. Music. Culture. We've got them all.

So get ready to push out your chest, proudly look the world in the eye, and say, "F*ck you, I'm Irish!"

The Humble Spud of Life, Death, and Exodus

The potato is inextricably linked not only with the Irish diet, but with the whole of Irish culture and history. However, potatoes were rarely seen in Ireland before British explorer Sir Walter Raleigh popularized them on his lands in the 1580s. The potato proved remarkably easy to cultivate in Ireland and packed an extraordinary nutritional punch, complete with protein, vitamins, and complex carbohydrates. The Irish wholeheartedly adopted this new wonder food. The typical Irish peasant ate about 10 pounds of potatoes each day and soon towered in physical size over their rural English equivalents who mainly ate bread.

Infant mortality declined dramatically among the Irish. From 1780 to 1840, the population doubled, zooming from 4 million to 8 million. There was one flaw: As much as 60 percent of the Irish people were solely dependent on the humble spud as their main food source. Then came the devastating blight—a malign misfortune that was to change the course of Ireland and the United States forever. This fast-growing fungus spurred mildew to form on all parts of the potato plant, causing entire fields to rot within days. To great dismay, the crops in 1845, 1846, and 1847 were decimated, leaving a vast quantity of the unfortunate Irish without any food or livelihood. This led to widespread death from starvation and disease, and mass exodus to the US.

It was a number of years before it was discovered that spraying the fields with a solution of copper sulfate effectively protected the potato crop. But by then, the horrific damage to the Irish population, economy, and culture had been done. Ireland would never fully recover from this dire catastrophe. Meanwhile, an ocean away, the US would grow and prosper like never before, thanks greatly to its new population of Irish immigrants.

Fighting Irish

There's incredible fire in the Irish temperament. Whether it's with a stinging verbal putdown or mean left hook, the Irish are not afraid to defend their homes, their families, and their rights. Just like Notre Dame's feisty leprechaun mascot, Irish immigrants became known in the New World for a refusal to give up and simply take no for an answer. Banging away at the slammed doors of Anglo-Saxon America's prejudice, this tough and fearless people kept trying—and fighting—until they overcame injustice and intolerance. Be it in the rough-and-tumble world of inner-city politics or the bare-knuckle boxing ring, the Irish rightly earned their fightin' moniker. These hard-as-nails immigrants weren't bickering over a few pints of Guinness or who insulted whose granny, they were battling for respect, freedom, and prosperity in their adopted country.

The Luck of the Irish

Sure, you've heard all about the Irish and their amazing luck. You've probably even bought lottery scratch cards festooned with shamrocks, leprechauns, rainbows, and pots of gold. Are the Irish any luckier than anybody else? Let's look at the evidence, shall we? Brutally oppressed by England, the Irish were forced to abandon their homeland in the millions, only to meet with poverty and "No Irish Need Apply" signs wherever they went. Mmm, the Irish variant of good fortune usually seems to be defined by "down on their luck." The concept of the Irish being blessed in any way could potentially be viewed as the cruelest joke ever.

Still, there is a certain Irish cussedness and willingness to take wild and crazy chances that may end up leading to lots of good fortune. And then there's the distinctive Irish exuberance and willingness to celebrate any incidence of random windfall. Maybe that's why everybody regarded the Irish as lucky. Anytime something did go right, they were up drinking and carrying on until the break of dawn.

So, maybe, we Irish are just more inclined to celebrate and share our good luck with all who are around when it occurs. Just hope you're lucky enough to be there the next time one of us hits it big.

St. Patrick's Day

The Sober Version

Before you start rubbing your hands in glee, anticipating riotous escapades involving dozens of cute colleens with skimpy green tops, glittery face paint, and barrels of green beer, know that St. Patrick's Day in Ireland was traditionally a quiet, church-oriented affair.

The typical Irish family would rise early and find a solitary sprig of shamrock to put on their somber Sunday best. Then they'd spend the morning in church listening to sermons of how thankful they should be that St. Patrick saved a bunch of ungrateful sinners. Nobody wore green, as it was considered an unlucky color not suitable for church. Fun stuff, eh? It gets better... Rather than spending the rest of the day gallivanting around the town square tossing green beads and asking complete strangers to smooch under the shamrocks, there was a quiet, sober parade promoting responsibility and community values, with no drunken shenanigans whatsoever. You see, St. Patrick's Day, Good Friday, and Christmas Day were the three days of the year when the pubs weren't allowed to open. Yep, you heard it right folks, the towns and villages of Ireland were dry as a rock in the desert on Ireland's national feast day. People generally just gathered for a hearty family meal somewhat like the US Thanksgiving feast, annoyed the hell out of each other, and had an early night.

Parading with Pride

Yep, the massive, spectacular parades attended by impressive crowds are an American innovation. The largest St. Patrick's Day parade in the US takes place in New York, where the event draws an average of 2 million people of all nationalities. The second-largest celebration is held in Boston. This South Boston Parade is probably the nation's oldest, first being hosted by the Charitable Irish Society of Boston all the way back in 1737. Another early March 17 celebration took place in New York City in 1762, when Irishman John Marshall held a celebration in his house. Little is known about the event except that guests apparently marched in a festive formation to his gathering.

The first organized modern New York parade was held in 1766 when military units strode at dawn from the house of one leading Irish citizen to the next. Over the years, as the parade grew in strength, it became a chance for the Irish to gather and demonstrate their combined political influence. Apart from showing that they were a force to be reckoned with, it was, of course, also a chance to blow off some steam and have "a grand old time." In its current incarnation, the parade is about Irish heritage—with the added benefit that everyone else gets a chance to join in and become "green" for the day. Meanwhile, back in Ireland, the parade has become "Americanized" in the last decade or two. Irish people now don the same kind of crazy getups that they do in the US.

CHAPTER 2

How the Irish Made America

While the Great Famine was a major motivation for Irish immigration to the United States, this movement was well under way prior to the famine and continued long after its effects had subsided. The main impetus for the mass migration was a potent combination of religious persecution, unfeasible rents, and the constant threat of eviction from the land. The treacherous and unreasonable nature of English rule had a lot to do with all of the aforementioned factors.

For a people who struggled under British control, the United States held an allure as the colony that had set itself free of imperial rule. Their desire to better themselves combined with abundant American opportunities meant that most Irish saw the US as a promised land.

From the birth of America to the modern day, the Irish have had a dynamic and far-reaching effect on the development of their adopted country. Often they've had to push their way through the doors of power. Having come so far and suffered so much, they were not going to be denied! Whether serving in the military, building industry, organizing politically, or making their way in any other part of American culture, the Irish were determined to create a free and prosperous life for themselves. This Irish-American struggle led to social and political progress for all Americans.

Fightin' for America

The Irish have played a part in every military conflict on American soil since the founding of the republic. Donegal-born Richard Montgomery was the first American general to lose his life in the Revolutionary War. In fact, one British major general at the time told the House of Commons that "half the rebel Continental Army was from Ireland."

Some 26 American generals either were born in Ireland or had Irish ancestry. A stand-out for her heroism and accomplishments in American military history was Lydia Barrington Darragh (1729–1789), born in Dublin, who spied for George Washington. Then there was brave Hercules Mulligan, a most resourceful spy in the American Revolution. Mulligan emigrated from Derry to New York City, where he led the Sons of Liberty in their famous assault on King George III's statue in Bowling Green. (They toppled it to the ground and melted its lead down for bullets to be used against the King's troops. Take that, symbol of British power!)

Mulligan stayed in the city during the British takeover, slyly pretending to be a loyalist himself. In secret he was listening intently to British soldiers' plans, since they often chatted in his clothing store. In this way Washington learned that British agents planned to kidnap him. After the Americans took control of the city, many accused Mulligan of being a Tory, but in 1783 Washington declared Mulligan "a true friend of liberty," which settled the matter. For his services to his adopted country, this courageous Irishman deserves to be remembered as "Mulligan the Mighty!"

John Barry (1745–1803), hailing from Wexford, is known as the "Father of the American Navy." He came to Philadelphia as a cabin boy of 15 and rose to become a captain. In the first Continental Navy he commanded the USS *Lexington* to become the first of the fleet to take a British ship. Recalled from private shipping after the war, he helped establish the young nation's new navy.

Moving forward in time, we have William J. Donovan (1883–1959), a World War I hero who later set up the Office of Strategic Services. Let's not forget General Douglas MacArthur (1880–1964), who led WWII's Allied forces in the Pacific. Finally, let's tip our hats to Audie Murphy (1925–1971), the most decorated US soldier in WWII, who in his second career as a popular movie actor fought the war again in many Hollywood movies.

Democracy, Power, and Political Machines

With our gift for language and willingness to stand up and be counted, as well as heaps of charm and charisma, we Irish have long been an integral part of American political life. The very first reading of the Declaration of Independence before Congress was a rousing rendition by none other than Charles Thomson, an Irish-born former indentured servant who rose to secretary of the Continental Congress.

Irish Catholics with experience in mass agitation movements against tyranny in their homeland realized that politics could provide a means for attaining influence and power. In the years after the Civil War, Irish clout in city politics became increasingly evident across the United States. Though subtle string-pulling and skillfully "playing the game" were undoubtedly vital to many of their political "machines" in New York and other cities, Irish politicians frequently helped the unemployed obtain jobs and organized other practical aid to the less fortunate.

In the rough-and-tumble sphere of New York City politics, the Irish fighting spirit was channeled through the massive Tammany Hall political machine. This largely Irish institution may not always have played by the rules, but times were tough and for a people fleeing famine and a repressive regime, bending the laws and rigging the game seemed a better option than waiting around for a fair deal to be handed to them on a plate. A few probably enriched themselves along the way, believing that in a dog-eat-dog world the only problem with tainted money is "tain't enough of it for everybody!"

While the machine's methods were not completely above board, it fought against entrenched political elites. And in their own way, Tammany politicians helped extend political power to the masses—making American democracy more inclusive of all its citizens.

A Hard Day's Work

It's often said that "the Irish built America." The truth is, not only did they build it, they also manufactured, repaired, and cleaned it, especially in the decades before and after the potato famine. As they were largely poor, unconnected, uneducated, and discriminated against, many unskilled Irish women and men found the strongest economic opportunities in industrial work, domestic service, and blue-collar public works positions. From 1850 onward, more and more immigrants got a head start in America in the form of welcoming relatives who provided moral support, a financial safety net, and whatever connections they might have had. Irish immigrants quickly found employment (mostly blue-collar) in the police and fire departments and other public institutions of the larger cities, due in some part to the influence of Irish political machines in the urban areas of the Northeast.

Toward the end of the 19th century, teaching became the sought-after occupation for a second generation of female Irish immigrants. By 1890, 40 percent of the go-getting second generation Irish in Boston held white-collar jobs.

Finally, through the growing network provided by Catholic colleges and the rapidly expanding system of public education, Irish Americans began to establish notable footholds in skilled professions like law and medicine. In 1903, Sir James Power, Lord Mayor of Dublin, was surprised to note on a transatlantic trip that the typical Irish immigrant in America was now "not merely a hewer of wood and a drawer of water." In fact, he remarked that they are "found occupying...respectable positions in society."

Women's Work in the New World

Rather surprising for such a dangerous venture, women made up over half of those departing from Ireland for America. They left a land where, frankly, women were undervalued within a strongly patriarchal society. Besides the usual household work, women often handled the family finances. Many were sent to cities to be shop assistants or carry out domestic work. With few prospects at home for single women (called "unprovided-for girls"), their families often saved to send them to America.

When audacious Irish women arrived in the States, they did not leave their knowledge and skills behind. They often gravitated to domestic work. Home workers were in great demand in wealthy, middle-class, and upper-middle-class homes in the 19th century. Armies of young Irish women found positions as live-in domestics. Imagine a world with few of the home conveniences we have today. Everything had to be done by hand. Even toast was made over an open fire. A servant's life was undoubtedly a hard one, yet with room and board provided for, many were able to save impressive sums, which they sometimes used to set up small businesses. In the 1870s it was estimated that a third of all the money in the Irish economy came from money sent by kindhearted Irish servant girls to their families. The Emigrant Industrial Savings Bank in New York alone would send more than $30 million to Ireland between 1850 and 1880. Many families in Ireland owed their survival to what they gratefully called the "American Letter," a lifeline that helped them cope with brutal poverty and lack of opportunity.

America's industrial revolution late in the century provided factory jobs, although the conditions there were often demeaning and downright dangerous. A significant number of women became nuns and made a powerful impact in society by increasing awareness and dedication to social needs. As the nation grew and the Irish community gained a foothold, Irish women entered a wider range of occupations such as office work, nursing, and teaching.

Mother Jones

The Irish have always believed in "a fair day's pay for a fair day's work." So it's no surprise they figured prominently in America's labor movement. Many Irish laborers were most certainly exploited as they built America. The struggle for workers' rights was heavily influenced by protest movements back in Ireland.

The most colorful labor activist of all time was Mother Jones. Born Mary Harris in Cork in 1837, she came relatively late to her vocation as organizer and agitator. Her life was marked by several harsh setbacks, including the death of her husband and four children in a yellow fever epidemic. After moving to Chicago, she lost all her possessions in the Great Chicago Fire.

At about this time, she became involved in union protests, joining the Knights of Labor. She was renowned as a dramatic orator who relished props, curses, and all kinds of attention-getting tactics—sound at all Irish to you? She exaggerated her age, referring to strikers not too much younger than herself as "my boys" and donning frumpish costumes to emphasize her "motherly" appearance. And we all know who wields the real power in an Irish household! Although she was dubbed "the most dangerous woman" in America, she was surprisingly conservative in some respects, not believing women's right to vote was worth fighting for, stating famously that "you don't need the vote to raise hell!" And raising hell was something Mother Jones knew how to do!

Westward Bound

Cattle occupied a central place in traditional Irish life for many centuries. In ancient times, the Irish were organized into tribes whose wealth and status were largely based on the size of their herds. Cattle were driven around with the tribe. Cattle rustling was a common way to get ahead and make one's fortune. With this history of cattle drives and rustling, it's not too surprising that a fair number of cowboys in the early West were Irish.

In the spring of 1844, Irishman Martin Murphy and his family members assembled with other homesteaders in Council Bluffs, Iowa. They were about to set off on an arduous 2,000-mile journey to seek a new life in California. Two previously attempted wagon trains had failed, only getting as far as the wilds of Nevada. This was long before the state had hotels or casinos. The Murphys bravely made the grueling journey and went on to become ranchers of vast holdings—with incredible numbers of cattle.

The Murphys weren't the only Irish to find their fortunes in the West. Far from it! Nellie Cashman, from Midleton, County Cork, made a mint providing "bed, board, and booze" to the gold and silver miners all over the western US and Canada. She was a prodigious entrepreneur, running and owning numerous stores, restaurants, and hotels in various mining settlements. While working the bar of her hotel, canny Nellie was able to buy a number of very lucrative mines by discreetly listening to the gossip of drunken prospectors. Along with her business savvy, Nellie had a reputation for incredible philanthropy, both toward individuals and Catholic charitable organizations. Among her many nicknames was "the Angel of Tombstone," a tribute to her extensive charitable endeavors there.

Irish history is littered with tales of misfortune and woe. Yet, once in a while, an event occurs that is so uplifting, so incredibly fortuitous that it makes you believe that there really is such a thing as the "luck of the Irish." Pull up a chair and listen to the amazing tale of the intrepid Irish lads who became rich mining the Comstock Lode in Nevada. The first two partners, Flood and O'Brien, were already co-owners in a prosperous Gold Rush saloon. In

1868, joined by James Fair and John Mackay, the Irish Four demonstrated that classic Irish persistence in the face of overwhelming odds, forming a partnership to purchase a part of the famed Comstock Lode. This was a claim that many considered to be unproductive. However, their willingness to tell common wisdom to go feck itself paid off. The Comstock Lode was far from dead and these "Silver Kings" became fabulously wealthy, extracting over $100 million of the lustrous metal from the mine. Who the hell needs a pot of gold at the end of a rainbow when you've got that?

Gone with the Irish Wind

Both the book and film version of *Gone with the Wind* have shaped many of our modern perceptions of the Old South. Yet the Irish elements of the story and the general Irish influence on Southern culture are often overlooked. Author Margaret Mitchell borrowed freely from elements of her own Irish background in creating the fictional O'Hara clan. Much of the tenacious and independently minded nature of Scarlett is modeled on Mitchell's spirited Irish aunts and grandmother.

Scarlett O'Hara's father, Thomas, is an Irish immigrant who names his plantation Tara, after the home of the High Kings in Ireland. In an appealing nod to the "luck of the Irish," we read that Thomas O'Hara won his lands in a card game! After Scarlett gently teases him for talking "like an Irishman," he states that he's proud to be Irish and imparts to her an Irish love of the land, saying that it's "the only thing in the world worth working for, worth fighting for, worth dying for, because it's the only thing that lasts."

His go-getting attitude is an understandable one for Irish Catholics who had escaped a cycle of insecurity and poverty as tenant farmers in their own country. In another acknowledgment of their Irish Catholic heritage, the

O'Haras are twice depicted saying the Rosary, a ritual that was a central part of many devout Irish-American households.

More than two-thirds of the Irish in the South lived in cities like New Orleans, Baltimore, Charleston, Richmond, Memphis, and Savannah. In New Orleans, St. Patrick's Day has been celebrated as far back as 1809, when throwing cabbages combined the Mardi Gras tradition of throwing objects into the crowd with the Irish love for the leafy vegetable. Savannah still holds one of the largest St. Patrick's Day parades in the United States.

Education for Every American

Educational achievement—plus heaps of hard work—have greatly helped successive generations of Irish Americans find financial rewards and professional prestige in their adopted country. Irish immigrants deftly balanced work and family obligations, scraping up money for school supplies to diligently acquire as much knowledge and as many qualifications as they could.

However, in the middle of the 19th century, New York clergyman "Dagger" John Hughes was troubled by negative perception of Catholics in the city's public school system. With typical Irish pluck, he decided to do something about it. Rallying together concerned individuals from all walks of life, he began a grassroots organization to fight this insidious anti-Catholic and anti-Irish prejudice. The program greatly boosted the development of Catholic parochial schools, which have always had a strong Irish flavor. Such church-run organizations provided high standards, a rigorous work ethic, and affordable and accessible schooling for generations of eager young minds at a time when a quality education was often seen as the exclusive privilege of the rich—something not to be "wasted" on ordinary working people. Catholic colleges began to provide higher education to Catholics who were not permitted to attend other institutions. Older illustrious Catholic colleges with strong Irish connections included Georgetown (1791) and St. Louis University (1818). Later in the 19th century, the number grew dramatically, with the advent of other fine schools such as Fordham (New York, 1841), Notre Dame (South Bend, Indiana, 1842), St. Joseph's University (Philadelphia, 1851), and the University of St. Mary of the Lake (Chicago, 1844).

Today, these Irish-influenced institutions comprise some of the most respected and powerful educational powerhouses in the US, offering both forward-looking innovation and the best of traditional scholarship. Of equal importance is the fact that Hughes's masterfully run campaign to educate the Irish paved the way for the secularization of public schools and started America on a path where public education was available for all.

Fitzgerald's Irish Tycoon

Irish immigrants may have made their name as laborers, domestic servants, and farmers, but there are many accounts of the Irish achieving great success and wealth. Although *The Great Gatsby* is an American classic from the pen of an Irish American writer, few realize that F. Scott Fitzgerald's "Great American Novel" revolves around one such Irish tycoon.

Through personal connections, Fitzgerald met self-made Irish immigrant millionaire Bourke Cochran. Fitzgerald went to lavish parties at The Cedars, Cochran's sprawling Long Island estate. Well, we all know how the Irish like to throw a lively shindig that lasts till dawn! At one such event Fitzgerald found himself in the midst of the society he would later depict in the novel. While the character of Gatsby is an amalgam, it's likely that Cochran was one of the main inspirations. From humble roots in

Sligo, Cochran came to the US at 18, and with true Irish grit and ingenuity went from rags to riches. He pulled himself up by his bootstraps to become a lawyer and made his fortune in the profession—millions per year in today's money. The iconic literary figure of Gatsby is perhaps a reflection of the hopes and dreams many Irish brought to the shores of America. Sadly, the talented but tormented author Fitzgerald himself died of an alcohol-related heart attack at age 44. The lure of the high-flying party lifestyle promised more than it could ever deliver. Still, like any true Irishman worth his salt, Fitzgerald entertained thousands along the way.

Rags to Railroad Riches

Money (or its lack) was one of the factors that drove so many struggling Irish to tearfully emigrate. Some of them, like Diamond Jim Bray, were catapulted to undreamt-of riches. One of the most colorful of the rags-to-riches characters of America's Gilded Age, James Buchanan Brady was born to a humble Irish-American family. Starting off as a bellhop and courier on the railroads, he quickly learned a great deal about the new means of transport. Brady made his pot of gold selling supplies to the railroad; he increased this fortune manifold with nimble speculation and bold investments. He was renowned for his enormous appetite, gregarious nature, and taste for good living—a lively lad by all accounts! His nickname came from his distinctive fondness for donning dazzling diamond jewelry festooned into fantastical forms and figures.

From Humble Origins to the White House

Mythical but far from fictional, the best example of the Irish rise in America is the Kennedy dynasty. Everyone knows the legend of John

Kennedy, from the power of his presidency to the tragedy of his assassination. Yet few know the humble origins of America's Camelot.

This famous and influential family traces its roots in America back to Bridget Murphy and her husband Patrick Kennedy, who arrived in Boston in 1849. When her husband died of cholera at the age of 35, the newly widowed Bridget found the strength and resourcefulness to provide for their four young children.

Mrs. Kennedy toiled as a domestic servant and used her savings to start a notions and stationery store, which she gradually and skillfully expanded. Bridget's hard work and sacrifice, making her way as a widow in a strange land, established the funds her son P. J. Kennedy used to finance his liquor business. This enterprise was to become the basis of the family's future progress and put Bridget's descendants on a path that dazzled America and forever changed the political scene.

CHAPTER 3

Hope and Heavy Hearts

It was America's good fortune that the Irish arrived upon its shore in large numbers. Back in Ireland, it was anything but good fortune that motivated the mass emigration. Poverty, starvation, and abuse at the hands of the English forced the desperate Irish to find a home where their hard work would benefit them instead of their colonial masters.

In the 19th century, approximately 8 million people left Ireland, the vast majority of whom went to the United States. Today, it's estimated that over 80 million people of Irish descent live outside Ireland—an astonishing 14 times more than the population of the island itself. Roughly 34 million Americans proudly reported Irish ancestry in the 2000 US Census.

It was not an easy decision to leave Ireland, nor a trouble-free journey to reach America. Both experiences were more horrific than anyone should face. Yet the Irish, with their resilient spirit, decided to make the best of the situation and bravely start over in the New World. Indeed, many people of Irish descent still retain a strong sense of their Irish heritage. So powerful is this bond and so devoted is the loyalty of the Irish diaspora that Article 2 of the Irish Constitution formally recognizes that "...the Irish Nation cherishes its special affinity with people of Irish ancestry living abroad who share its cultural identity and heritage."

Black '47

The Great Famine of 1845–51 was perhaps the most serious disaster in Irish history, with long aftereffects and wide-ranging impact. A vast number of survivors emigrated, many of them to the United States. As many as 1.5 million individuals who remained died of starvation and various epidemics that followed in the famine's wake. It was a ghastly time, but the Irish bore this hideous misfortune with incredible strength.

The most shocking aspect of the famine is the fact that although many were starving, there was plenty of food in Ireland. The island grew more than 1 billion pounds of grain every year. However, most of this was sold and exported so that tenant farmers could have the money to pay rent. Ireland was prohibited from importing wheat or rice from the British colonies until the entire British crop was sold at higher prices than the colonial foodstuffs.

By the time that famine reached its height in 1847 ("Black '47," as people called it), public relief was being distributed, but only in return for 12-hour days of intensive physical labor. This further weakened many already racked by hunger and disease. That winter was an exceptionally bitter one, and the workers had to toil in rags—adding insult to their shivering injury.

Most unfortunate of all was the fact that such public works projects meant many farmers didn't have enough time to plant crops. That made the following year's harvest worse than it should have been. As the final straw, many of these public projects were clearly pointless—walls that didn't protect anything and roads that led nowhere.

The fact that exports to Britain of foods such as meat, butter, grains, and vegetables continued throughout the famine was a cause of much bitterness—at the time and up to the present day. But the famine became another proof that Ireland could not be destroyed, and it set the stage for the Irish people's determination to control their own destiny.

Coffin Ships

Numerous brave Irish immigrants faced and overcame incredible challenges. For instance, many of the passengers in the years during and immediately after the Great Famine came on board so-called coffin ships. These were incredibly unsafe vessels with dire overcrowding, poor sanitation, and meager starvation rations. Often weakened by hunger and disease before the voyage, many died on board, where mortality rates of 20 percent were relatively common—even reaching 50 percent in some instances. It's an indication of how hopeless the conditions were in Ireland—and how fearless these immigrants were—that any of them even considered such a journey.

The fare to America was often paid by landlords of tenant farmers, as they had become responsible for the cost of keeping any destitute ex-tenants in the poorhouse. Heartless and cruel calculations indicated that mass transportation of unfortunate Irish to America in floating death traps was cheaper than paying to keep them at subsistence level in their homeland. Ill-fated passengers who died on the way were callously tossed overboard. Horrific eyewitness accounts tell of sharks following the ships in anticipation of a steady supply of corpses.

Apart from the discomfort, life onboard was very bleak, with only occasional sightings of other ships or sea creatures to break the monotony. Storms were grueling ordeals and rather frequent. Passengers suffered from exhaustion and hunger-induced weakness. Crowding and unsanitary conditions led to the rapid spread of disease, including typhoid. In cases of illness, there was rarely a doctor on board. It's a testament to the Irish tenacity and determination that such intrepid souls not only survived the voyage but went on to thrive in their new homeland.

Hardship and Homesickness

The lot of 19th century Irish immigrants was a tough one. Fleeing from oppression at home, they often faced discrimination on American shores. When they left home, family and friends usually held poignant "American wakes," reflecting the harsh reality that the emigrants would in all likelihood never be seen alive again.

Once in the US, thousands crowded seedy New York slums like Sweeney's Shambles and the notorious Five Points. In these rundown areas, crime and violence ran rampant. High mortality rates and economic insecurity, plus the temptations and challenges of a massive, teeming city, made it tough to keep families intact. Sicknesses like tuberculosis (which Bishop Hughes called the "natural death of the Irish immigrants") carried off many dwelling in severely unhealthy conditions. Families suffered from the abandonment or early death of male heads of the household. In the 1840s and 1850s an estimated 50,000 unfortunate Irish women entered prostitution to survive. All this had its fallout. A study showed that between 1849 and 1859, two-thirds of immigrants entering the city's mental hospital on Blackwell's Island were Irish. Sometimes, dashed hopes created a deep and powerful longing for the old country. But the Irish, as always, transformed the worst of experiences and eventually overcame these tragic setbacks. Yet melancholy reminders of these tough times linger in countless Irish songs and stories. Even though they suffered and were often mistreated, the Irish maintained their desire to hold tight to their culture through thick and thin. As they established themselves and created new lives and institutions, they steadfastly retained a sense of where they'd come from and what their culture meant to them.

Shanty and the "Gentleman Who Pays the Rent"

The word shanty comes from the Gaelic *sean tí*, meaning old house. With little capital or education to establish themselves in their new homeland, many Irish emigrants to the US were forced to squeeze into rundown, overcrowded neighborhoods with extremely poor housing conditions. These soon became known as shanty towns, and those who lived there were commonly dubbed "shanty Irish" to distinguish them from the more prosperous "lace curtain" Irish who had set about beautifying their dwellings in the form of upmarket window dressings and other refinements. However, for many Irish stuck in the tenements, especially in the decades immediately following the Great Famine, lack of connections and rampant discrimination meant they had to use whatever means possible to keep body and soul together. Always resourceful and looking for a way to make something out of nothing, many shanty Irish continued the rural tradition of keeping pigs. These hungry hogs could forage among the leftovers and garbage in the streets, growing gradually into an asset the family could sell or even feast upon. This urban livestock was commonly referred to as "the gentleman who pays the rent." The presence of these roving beasts might have shocked other Americans at the time. Since then, we've learned that pigs are highly intelligent and sociable creatures— and the notion of fattening animals with waste products would now be regarded as highly ecological. Of course, it could also be said that the shanty Irish were just decades ahead of the whole recent trend of keeping Vietnamese pot-bellied pigs as pets.

Post-Famine Ireland

The Great Famine was the worst disaster in all of Ireland's sad and unfortunate history. It's estimated that over 1 million people died and more than 1 million emigrated, so that Ireland's population decreased from 8 million to 6 million in a few short and devastating years. Father Paul Cullen, who became Archbishop of Armagh in 1849, regarded the famine as a divine punishment intended to purify the Irish people, whom Cullen believed were still too attached to pre-Christian superstitions and customs. So participation in Catholic sacraments like attending Mass saw a great resurgence. This wasn't the only change afoot. Marriages were delayed until later in life so that people could save enough to provide for a family. The impoverished Irish were reluctant to take financial risks after the complete devastation they had witnessed all around them. Irish speakers abandoned their native tongue as they wished to be fluent in English for life in their future homelands. By 1851, the typical farm grew to 30 acres or more. Fathers stopped subdividing acreage among their sons and instead bequeathed the whole property to just one—usually the eldest. It became accepted that younger brothers would have to emigrate, many to North America. This loss of young energetic go-getters meant there were few risk-takers to build new businesses. Ireland's loss would turn out to be America's gain as many Irish worked hard and prospered in their new home—enriching its economic and cultural life as they did so.

CHAPTER 4

Bloody Ingenious

Necessity is the mother of invention, and if ever there were a people with needs, it was the Irish. So it's no surprise that the Irish innovated their way right into the 21st century. Today, Ireland's economy has expanded far beyond cattle rearing and dairy farming into everything from tropical fruits to microchips. Companies such as Irish-owned and -based Fyffes perfectly showcase modern Irish ingenuity. Fyffes is the fourth-largest banana distribution company in the world, importing the entire production of Belize into Ireland then moving it onward to the rest of Europe. Yes, a kelly green company provides Europe with this famously yellow fruit. Meanwhile, Ireland's technology sector continues to thrive, manufacturing 25 percent of Europe's computers and ranking as the world's largest exporter of software. Microsoft, Apple, IBM, and Dell have all claimed a corner of the loveliest land on earth. But this modern wave of innovation is nothing new. The Irish have a long and proud history of inventiveness.

Colors of the Rainbow

Songs and poems have been written about the colors of Ireland—its 40 shades of green, the flaming red hair of its colleens, and the deep, dark blue of its windswept seas. It's fitting that it was an Irishman who invented modern color photography in all its multihued glory. In 1894, John Joly from County Offaly discovered the first quick, convenient method to capture rich, vibrant colors on film—from one single plate. Finally, people could easily capture and preserve the vibrancy of everyday life. The Irish Tourist Board and millions of visitors to Ireland are forever in Joly's debt. In true Irish fashion, he didn't rest on his laurels. Not merely content with changing how we saw the world, the Offaly man also invented the photometer for measuring the intensity of light—as well as the strength of radiation used in cancer treatment.

Me Feet Are Killing Me

When it comes to Irish footwear, one's inclined to think of the solid, hefty boots of honest farmers and workmen. Or those fine leather slippers used for the intricate acrobatics of Irish step dancers. Sneakers don't really spring to mind as being particularly Irish. However, the sneaker as we now know it would be impossible without rubber heels—and these were the result of some classic Irish resourcefulness. This comfortable and life-enhancing innovation—beloved by athletes and, of course, all those who stand on their feet while working—dates from 1899 when Cork-born Humphrey O'Sullivan attached some rubber to his shoes to make standing all day more comfortable for his aching feet.

O'Sullivan toiled hard and long in a print shop in Lowell, Massachusetts. At first he stood on a rubber mat to ease his discomfort. Unfortunately, his coworkers kept "borrowing" his mat and poor O'Sullivan was forced to replace it constantly. Not one to let a minor misfortune get him down, the ingenious Humphrey came up with the idea of attaching a rubber heel to his shoes. Savvy O'Sullivan patented the idea and founded his own highly successful company, which over 100 years later still trades today as the O'Sullivan Corporation.

Green Ink

Anybody who's ever had a Celtic cross, Claddagh, tricolor, or other symbol of their Irishness etched boldly on their person owes a debt of gratitude to Irish immigrant and New York tattooist Samuel O'Reilly. In 1891, this artistic and inventive fellow filed the first US patent for an electric tattoo machine based on the rotary technology of Thomas Edison's automatic pen. Little is known about the skintastic Samuel—a major void in the annals of tattoo history. However, it seems O'Reilly was sought after by show-business types who valued his artistic skill, the clarity of his work, and the speed at which he operated.

Plying his trade on the Bowery and later in the back of a barber's shop at 11 Chatham Square, it would be interesting to know if O'Reilly created any Irish-inspired designs, but tattooing in those days was a very underground activity and few records were kept by those practicing this inky art form. The late, great Mr. O'Reilly died in relative obscurity in 1908. Reports say he fell off a ladder while painting his house in Brooklyn—not a bad way for a practical Irishman to go! His legend as inventor and artist lives on in the names of tattoo shops in several states. It's worth noting that tattooing and body painting were practiced by the ancient Celts in Ireland. Their warriors traditionally charged naked into battle screaming ferociously at their enemies, daubed with blue paint and tattooed with mystical patterns. This appearance gave them courage—and no doubt scared the bejesus out of their opponents! So next time your Auntie Bridget gives you hell about your tats, your loudness, and your argumentative behavior, tell her you're just continuing a very old and esteemed Irish tradition!

Highways and Byways

The Irish have always been a restless and mobile race—eager to move on and set off on adventure. It's hardly surprising that they have been associated with trade routes and modes of transport of various kinds. In ancient Ireland, major towns were linked by surprisingly advanced ancient roads which generally ran along the tops of gravelly hills known as eskers. The most important was the Esker Riada, a system of ridges that stretch across the narrowest point of Ireland, between Dublin and Galway. This series of hilltop roads was of course far less speedy than the world's first suburban commuter railway that opened between Dublin and Dun Laoghaire in 1834 (two years before the London and Greenwich Railway).

Nowadays, we take widespread ownership of cars for granted. However, in the opening decades of the 20th century, the motor car was seen as a rich man's toy, something along the lines of a private jet or motorboat today. Henry Ford, the son of an Irish tenant farmer from County Cork, was the first to conceive of and make the car available to a mass market. Now in 21st-century Ireland, decades after cars and motorway construction became commonplace, there are still plenty of windy roads, including a network of quaint "boreens." The boreen is a narrow road that was traditionally just wide enough to turn a cow around on—important in a country where cattle need to be moved from one part of a fragmented farm to the other or brought to a marketplace in a nearby town. As a stubborn Irish farmer might put it, "Where there's a will there's a way to get there!"

Hoban's House

America's most famous landmark was the illustrious creation of an enterprising Irish immigrant. Born in a humble cottage in County Kilkenny, James Hoban began his working life as a wheelwright and carpenter until his exceptional talent as a draftsman was recognized when he received a place at the Dublin Society's Drawing School. There he excelled and was granted a medal for his drawing of "Brackets, Stairs, and Roofs."

At a time when many Irish immigrants lived in crowded shanty towns, this architectural master became responsible for one of America's grandest and most recognizable residences, none other than the White House itself. Hoban immigrated to the US after the Revolutionary War. Through talent and exceptional crafts-manship, he established himself as an archi-tect in Philadelphia. During a stint in South Carolina, Hoban worked on notable structures like the Charleston County Courthouse and several gentlemen's mansions in the surround-ing region. On a tour of the South, George Washington was struck by Hoban's exceptional handiwork, and in 1792, Hoban won the con-test to design the White House. Even though few of his other buildings have survived, James Hoban's White House remains one of the world's most distinctive architectural landmarks—and a symbol of America.

Mr. Murphy's Bed

Irish Americans always had a knack for mak-ing the most of whatever they had. Like many before them, William L. Murphy and his wife lived in cramped conditions with little space for entertaining. In their tiny one-room apartment in San Francisco, not even the little people could fit inside for tea and a visit! To solve their cramped dilemma, Mr. Murphy started playing with the mechanics of a folding bed. In 1900, he applied for a patent and created the Murphy Door Bed Company. The firm went through ups and downs over the following decades. Unlike his beds, Murphy's company did not fold up. Fortunes picked up again in the 1970s and have continued an upward trend to this day. The Murphy Bed Company remains a family business, still run by the founder's grandson, Clark Murphy.

Water for Mr. Mulholland

William Mulholland, after whom Los Angeles's majestic Mulholland Drive is named, was born in Belfast in 1855. This adventurous young lad worked aboard ships making transatlantic crossings, eventually settling in California in 1876. He started his illustrious career in the US as a ditch digger with the Los Angeles Water Company, but with typical Irish pluck he soon climbed out of those ditches to make his mark on his adopted city. After work, he studied engineering and hydraulics long into the night. He rapidly rose to become superintendent of the water company. It was Mulholland who daringly proposed building a 240-mile aqueduct from the Sierra Nevada to LA. This complex system, completed between 1909 and 1913, allowed the City of Angels to boom. Otherwise, LA's current status as a vast metropolis would surely have withered on the vine. We wonder if Mulholland ever found it ironic that his career focused on searching a desert for water, an element so very abundant back in his native land.

Other Incredible Irish Firsts

A Castlebar man, Louis Brennan emigrated to Australia, where he found work as a watchmaker. However, he is not best known for his timepieces but for a device which was decidedly ahead of his time—a steerable torpedo. No Irishman worth his salt would give the British such an innovative weapon for free, but Brennan went above and beyond his entrepreneurial duty, selling the patent to the British navy for the then-phenomenal sum of £100,000, believed to be the largest amount ever paid for a patent up until then.

In 1879, the 4th Earl of Rosse installed a water wheel–powered turbine on his estate to provide electricity not just to Birr Castle but the town as well, making Birr, County Offaly, the first town in the world to be lit by electricity.

John Philip Holland invented the first fully operational submarine vessel in 1877. He went on to develop the first submarines used by the US Navy (1900), the Royal Navy (1901), and the Japanese Imperial Navy (1904).

In an attempt to better understand that fearsome orb responsible for burning many a fair Irish cheek, the astronomer William Edward Wilson became the first person to measure the temperature of the sun. All the way back in 1899, he estimated it at a sizzling 6590°C, impressively close to the modern value of 6075°C.

Owing to its geographic position at the western edge of Europe, Ireland played a key role in the development of long-distance communications with North America. In 1907, Irish-Italian inventor Guglielmo Marconi made sure his countrymen's gift of gab wouldn't be limited by something as piddling as an ocean and established the first permanent transatlantic radio transmitter near Cliffden, County Galway.

Leave it to an Irishman not to settle for just chatting with his neighbors down the lane.

CHAPTER 5

From Guinness to Whisk-e-y

It's true, the fun-loving Irish enjoy an *occasional* hard drink and have a reputation for starting all kinds of mischief after a few too many pints or shots. But in typical Irish fashion, they truly enjoy sharing their wonderful beverages with the rest of the world. Walk into any Irish bar and you'll quickly learn this lesson. Be it with spiked coffee, dark beer, or the smoothest of whiskeys, the Irish deserve plenty of credit for showing the world how a couple of drinks at a neighborhood bar can bring people together and transform strangers into friends.

Guinness

James Joyce once called Guinness stout "the wine of Ireland." Indeed it's one of the most successful beers worldwide. Ten million glasses of this ambrosial liquid are consumed with great gusto each day. If you ask for "a pint" in Ireland—unless you absolutely specify otherwise—it is assumed you want a pint of Guinness. Right from the beginning, Guinness intended on sticking around and making a lasting mark on the culture.

The original Guinness Brewery in Dublin has a 9,000-year lease on its property at a perpetual rate of IR£45 per year—one of the best bargains in Irish commercial history! Guinness is still the best-selling alcoholic drink in Ireland, where Guinness & Co. makes almost €2 billion annually—an impressive figure on an island with about 5 million inhabitants.

The Guinness harp motif is based on the Trinity College Harp. It was adopted in 1862 by the then proprietor, Benjamin Lee Guinness. When Guinness registered their harp as a trademark shortly after the Trade Marks Registration Act passed in 1875, they made sure that the harp faced right instead of left to differentiate it from the Irish coat of arms.

Guinness drinkers are very insistent that their pints be dispensed correctly. Anything else would be a crime! A proper pint of Guinness should have a thick head of foam on top. To get this right, the bartender pours the draft into the pint, lets it sit for three or four minutes, then tops it off for serving. Like so many of the good things in life, a well-poured pint of Guinness is worth waiting for.

Fluthered, Banjaxed

Where certain phenomena are common it is usual to have a multiplicity of synonyms that describe them. We've all heard about the Inuit having an incredible variety of words to describe snow, making a host of subtle distinctions between icy precipitation that occurs at certain times or that has certain physical characteristics. Likewise, we Irish have more than a word or two to describe various states of inebriation. Well, we're sociable people after all—and our top-class beers and whiskeys are far too tempting to resist! A silver-tongued Irish reveler might use the word *fluthered* to describe being "merry," visibly not sober but in relatively good form with a capacity to function logically, if slightly exuberantly and eccentrically. *Banjaxed* implies a certain impairment to physical function—missing things, spilling drinks, and slurring words that would normally come tripping off the tongue. Even if you don't get a chance to use any of these words about yourself, we know you'll get a chance to use one about one of your Irish friends at some stage during your acquaintance.

Poitin

Also spelled *poteen* or *potcheen*, Ireland's traditional home-distilled spirit is notorious. It was typically made in a still shaped like a small pot (*poit* in Gaelic). Adding "een" to the end of a word in Gaelic denotes a degree of affection. Given the Irish fondness for strong liquor, we'd say there was a great friendliness toward this fiery homemade libation. However, home distillation has been illegal in Ireland since those mean-spirited (pun totally intended!) Brits banned it in the 17th century.

The resourceful Irish distilled from a wide array of substances, including various grains, treacle, potatoes, or dairy by-products. Basically, whatever you happened to have available on the farm went into the poit. Over the centuries, a whole outlaw culture has grown up around poitin. It was originally made over a turf fire, and the murky smoke was a dead giveaway to local law enforcement. Therefore, poitin stills were carefully relocated to remote areas, where were fired up on blustery windy days when the smoke would dissipate rather than sending signals to watchful policemen.

To avoid legal repercussions, stills were normally set up on the boundaries of various farmers' properties so it wouldn't be clear who was to blame! As with any illicit spirits, quality can vary widely, so people generally only buy from people they know, or "somebody who knows somebody who knows somebody." Fans of the ferociously intense liquid will shake the bottle to see if the rosary beads (a linked row of bubbles) form at the top. However, unscrupulous merchants have taken to adding bleach to produce the same effect! If you ever find yourself craving some of this fiendish concoction when you're in Ireland, it would be safer to stick to commercially produced legal versions that have become available in recent years. Loss of sight is said to be one of the outcomes of a bad batch of poitín—this gives a whole new meaning to the term "blind drunk"! Poitín was frowned upon by the Catholic Church, which made its manufacture grave enough of a sin to require a bishop's absolution rather than that of the regular parish priest. Ah, the lengths the Irish will go to for "the demon drink!"

Gaelic Coffee

Gaelic coffee (fancier than calling it just Irish) is basically Irish whiskey poured into hot java, which is then stirred with sugar and heaped with heavy cream on top. As we Irish might say, it both "revives and relaxes"—and it tastes delicious too. The concoction was invented by one Joe Sheridan, a head chef in Foynes, County Limerick, the precursor to Shannon

Airport. One dreadful winter night in the '40s a bedraggled group of Americans climbed out of a Pan Am aquatic plane (yes, they landed them on the water back then). Our resourceful barman Joe spiked the coffee with whiskey to defrost their bones. Some wondered aloud if they were drinking Brazilian coffee, and the witty Joe told them it was "Irish coffee." The world has been grateful ever since. It now had yet another way to enjoy Ireland's delectable whiskies. *San Francisco Chronicle* travel writer Stanton Delaplane (now there's a name suited to the job) partook of the concoction at Shannon and whisked the idea back to San Francisco's Buena Vista Café, where it was first served in 1952. Cracking the secret of the floating cream proved difficult. Feverish hours were spent, mistakes were made and drunk. San Francisco mayor George Christopher, who just happened to own a dairy, thought that cream aged at least two days would be more buoyant, and so it was. Delaplane gave the drink some ink in his columns, and a legend of Irish drink-lore gained worldwide renown—alongside the many other delightful beverages of Irish origin.

A Seriously Old-School Watering Hole

Sean's Bar on Main Street, Athlone, on the West Bank of the River Shannon, claims to be the oldest pub in Ireland, dating back to AD 900. The bar holds records of every owner since its opening, including gender-bending pop sensation Boy George (born George Alan O'Dowd to an Irish family originally from County Tipperary), who owned the premises briefly in 1987. Now tall tales are a dime a dozen, especially regarding local bragging rights, but in this case, the claims of Sean's Bar turn out to be more than just hot air. In 1970, renovations revealed the walls of the bar to be made of wattle and wicker dating back to the 10th century, lending credence to its legendary status, and in 2004, it received a certificate from Guinness World Records validating its claim as the "oldest public house in Ireland."

Pubs Across the Sea

Traditional Irish pubs do of course sell alcohol, but they also serve as restaurants, meeting places, offices, shops, and venues for traditional Irish music. Echoes of the Irish pub were found in the numerous Irish-owned and operated saloons that proliferated in the US up to Prohibition—and indeed afterward. All over the world, people have lifted a glass of good ale or fine whiskey in an Irish pub.

In New York City, for example, McSorley's, the oldest continuously operating saloon, is, naturally, Irish. Their natural conviviality and willingness to talk their asses off with anyone seems to have served Irish Americans well as they grew businesses built on *craic, caint, agus ceol* (good times, conversation, and music) thousands of miles from home. In matters of hospitality, Ireland takes the lead in more ways than one. For example, in 2002, Ireland was the first country in the world to introduce a public smoking ban. Skeptics at that time doubted that the law-bending Irish would ever abide by the ban, but it has been almost universally accepted.

Speakeasy Nights

When Prohibition cast its long, dark shadow across the American landscape, few were more willing to do their part to give the people what they wanted by keeping the booze flowing than the Irish. Thousands gained success in the often deadly business of producing, distributing, and serving illegal alcohol. The history books chronicling those days are dotted with such infamous Irish underworld names as George "Bugs" Moran, Jack "Legs" Diamond, and Dean

O'Bannion. True to their Celtic heritage, many of these lawbreakers were larger-than-life figures who loved drama and excitement. None was more saucy, in-your-face, and likeable than Mary Louise Cecilia Guinan, commonly known as "Tex" after her home state of Texas.

Before finding fame as the premiere celebrity of the Prohibition era, this wild and wacky Irish-American gal had worked as a bronco rider and an actor in Hollywood Westerns. Like many of her countrymen, Tex knew how to throw a rip-roarin' party. This fair colleen soon opened her own nightclub, the Salon Royale on Manhattan's West 48th Street. The glittery hotspot reflected Tex Guinan's irreverent Irish personality, offering music, showgirls, and rivers of illegal hooch. "Hello, sucker" was her usual devil-may-care greeting. Arrested constantly then beating the rap every single time, she boldly wore a necklace of tiny padlocks, one for every time the cops booked her. Ironically, her downfall came in the form of Irish American Mayor Jimmy Walker. When the club kicked out one of his cronies, he closed her down for good. Sadly but fittingly, Tex died two days before the end of Prohibition, in November of 1933.

Whisk-e-y

The glories of Irish whiskey have been justly celebrated in songs, extensively praised in literature, and enjoyed in vast quantities the world over. If you're serious about your liquor—and we Irish absolutely are—then there's only one kind of firewater you'd consider: the Irish kind! Our native tipple is distilled *three* times instead of two, purifying it and making it slightly sweeter, so when you take a sip, it's just like an angel crying on your tongue! To be certain you're consuming the real deal, look carefully at the label. W-h-i-s-k-e-y indicates the heavenly liquid from the Emerald Isle. Without the "e," it's from Scotland or some other godforsaken place.

Irish whiskey has been experiencing a golden age recently, with new blends and flavors continually appearing to tantalize the palate. Six whiskey distilleries are currently active in Ireland, including the world's oldest, Bushmills, which was founded in Antrim all the way back in 1608. In 2013, the market leader Jameson had annual sales topping an astounding 48 million bottles. Overall sales of Irish whiskey in the US are now about four times higher than they were a decade ago. At the rate it's going, this amber nectar might replace drinking water before too long—quite fitting as the word "whiskey" is derived from the Gaelic *uisce beatha,* meaning "water of life."

CHAPTER 6

Irish Pop Culture and Its Worldwide Impact

Whether it's because we're natural show-offs or just relish fun and good times, we Irish love showbiz. Our involvement with show business stretches all the way back to Vaudeville and Tin Pan Alley. Performers of Irish extraction found ways to turn hardship into humor and an outsider's perspective into mainstream entertainment. In all areas of the entertainment world, including acting, comedy, and music, many of our number have left an oversized mark. But the Irish influence on pop culture reaches far beyond our famous celebrities, with traditional Irish dance, musical instruments, and even charming jewelry finding their way onto America's stages, airways, and fingers.

Oscar-Worthy Irish

We Irish are no strangers to the silver screen. In fact we seem to be everywhere you turn. Irish directors such as Neil Jordan and Jim Sheridan rack up box office hits and critical acclaim. When it comes to acting, talented stars from James Cagney and Jack Nicholson to Saoirse Ronan and Mia Farrow have lit up the silver screen. It should be no wonder then that the "Oscar" statuette presented each year at the Academy Awards was designed by Dublin-born Cedric Gibbons, who was considered MGM's top set designer during Hollywood's heyday. Besides designing the coveted Oscar, Gibbons even managed to win a dozen of them for himself. As they say in Ireland (and elsewhere!), nice work if you can get it!

Bono

Few rock stars have made more of an impact or stayed in the charts as long as Dublin-born Bono has. While the former Dublin schoolboy possesses plenty of originality, a way with a tune, and a huge heap of showmanship, he's also made a mighty impact over the years as a force for positive change. From his early involvement with Band Aid, his philanthropic work has expanded over the years.

It's no wonder that Bono means "good" in Latin. This fiercely loyal family man and his wife, Ali Hewson, are major figures in the world of international philanthropy. Is he a rock star or a goodwill ambassador? Should he play music or go out to save people in need? The man can pull off both roles—with spadefuls of style and a certain strength of purpose. He and U2 have 22 Grammys between them, for the love of God!

Riverdance

Irish dancing has become a much-admired, innovative, and widely practiced artform. Yet, once upon a time, Irish dancing was all about comely lads and maidens hopping and skipping, with just an occasional bit of hardcore twirling and leaping to liven things up. It's no coincidence that Irish dancing classes were held in parish halls and church basements. There was no more respectable hobby for boys and girls of Irish heritage.

Over time, the US became the center of the Irish dancing universe. With good old American innovation and a quest for something different, the Irish kept pushing the envelope in terms of costumes, fancy footwork, and elaborately high hairdos. Still, even though the more advanced routines were so athletic they'd make a Connemara pony sweat, Irish dancing remained quiet and sedate, confined to the insider track of the corned beef and cabbage circuit. Then, in 1994, as part of Ireland hosting the Eurovision song contest, Irish American dancers and choreographers Michael Flatley and Jean Butler changed the Irish dancing world in a swirl of kick-ass tapping, thunderous synchronized beats, and enough glitz and glamour to make a topless Vegas showgirl blush. The sleepy little pastime had gone Hollywood. Mixing in influences from flamenco and tango, the whole tempo changed from a tippity-tappety snoozefest all the way to roller derby with Celtic costumes, dry ice, and flames.

In a way, Riverdance has taken Irish dancing back to its roots. In the 17th century, when Sir Henry Sidney, Queen Elizabeth's lieutenant in Ireland, saw Irish dancing in Galway, he commented on the "very beautiful, magnificently dressed, and first-class dancers." He noted that elaborate displays of Irish dancing were part of all important occasions, especially for visiting dignitaries; Sir Sidney would have loved Riverdance!

Hollywood: The Saintly Irish Version

There's no Sunset Strip in the tiny West Wicklow village called Hollywood, nor are there many people lounging poolside waiting to be discovered—they'd probably die of hypothermia in the chilly Wicklow air! However, you may find an occasional movie star and a few American accents in the vicinity. The craggy Irish countryside nearby is a popular location for top film shoots and has been the setting for such blockbusters as *Dancing at Lughnasa*, *Michael Collins*, and *King Arthur*. The American visitors to the village are largely tourists stopping to have their picture taken in front of the Hollywood post office.

The town's name dates back to at least the 12th century and is a corruption of "Holy Wood"; local hermit St. Kevin spent hours in prayerful contemplation among the groves of trees that still dot the landscape. Is there a connection between the picturesque home of a devout Irish saint and the entertainment world's bustling capital of sin and hucksterism? Locals recount that Michael Guirke, a young man who left the area after the potato famine, eventually found his fortune running a racetrack near Los Angeles, so it's possible that there was a direct link between the future home of the movie industry and this sleepy little spot nestled deep in the Wicklow hills.

Liam Neeson: Bad-Ass Action Hero

A tall and striking presence, Antrim native Liam Neeson is perhaps Ireland's best-known and well-established film actor. It seems that his first foray at age 11 into drama wasn't necessarily due to any great love of the art, but rather a chance to impress and get close to a girl he had a crush on. Such a romantic little fella, our Liam! His path toward becoming an actor was not a straightforward one. Along the way, he spent time studying physics and computer science in Belfast, then working at the Guinness brewery and briefly playing professional soccer. He also spent two years in England at a teacher-training college. Talk about brains and brawn! His first stint as an actor was with Lyric Players Theatre in Belfast in 1976, followed by a period in Dublin at the Abbey Theatre, the national theater of Ireland. In 1980 he was cast by John Boorman as Sir Gawain in *Excalibur*. After several successful films, he moved to Hollywood full-time in 1987. Despite his impressive career and host of awards, Neeson is known for an unaffected and down-to-earth, very Irish demeanor that endears him to fans and fellow professionals alike.

Colin Farrell: Ireland's Bad-Boy Heartthrob

The favorite Irish male movie star of recent years combines many typically Irish characteristics, appealing to a wide range of audiences as a result. For the mammies, he's got a sufficient amount of the "little boy lost." For the fellas, Colin is good-looking enough to attract a fair number of fine females to join your group. But at the same time, he's not "too full of himself." Colin gives the impression that he'd be up for "a good evening's craic and carousing." For the ladies, he's real enough to be one of your brother's good-looking (OK, let's make that really good-looking) friends. He's dreamy enough to fantasize over but not so unattainable as to make snaring him completely out of the question for an ordinary girl. With a decent amount of drunken escapades and sexy shenanigans to his name, he's good copy for the journalists. All in all, the perfect approachable-yet-slightly-unattainable mix that makes for long-lasting film stardom. Then there's the accent—down-to-earth Dub with a slight hint of badness.

Rings from the Claddagh

The Claddagh is a sleepy fishing settlement at the edge of Galway. Among the Claddagh customs was the use of a betrothal and wedding ring comprised of two hands (for friendship), a heart (for love), and a crown (for loyalty). Although closely associated with the Claddagh and Galway in general, similar rings have been found in other parts of Europe. So how did they make their way to the Claddagh? By some accounts, a 17th-century Galway man, Richard Joyce, was captured aboard a pirate ship and taken to North Africa's Barbary Coast. During his enforced servitude he acquired the trade of a goldsmith and learned the distinctive pattern that was to become the Claddagh ring, which he popularized as a free man back in his home city. Whatever its origins, this distinctive style of jewelry has become a popular symbol of Irish identity and pride. Its distinctive pattern has been incorporated into everything from earrings to bracelets, not to mention T-shirts and baseball caps. It's astonishing how a symbol from one tiny Irish fishing village has spread far and wide across the globe.

Bodhrán

Pronounced *bough-rawn,* this handheld drum with a tongue-twisting name was traditionally made of goatskin. Nowadays the material can often be a synthetic substitute. Between 10 and 26 inches in diameter, the *bodhrán* is played either with the hand or a beater (also known as a tipper or cipín), which drummers modeled from a knucklebone. The musician places a hand behind the skin to adjust the reverberation and overall tone of the instrument.

Although it might look traditional, the bodhrán has only shown up everywhere since the 1950s. Before then, it was used rarely, in remote communities. Traditional or not, its rolling, robust rhythm adds an extra dimension to the music of any group of Irish musicians. While they are required to keep strictly to the beat of the music they accompany, individual bodhrán players often add beats or distinctive extra notes. This improvisational quality makes the bodhrán a favorite at spontaneous "trad" sessions in Irish pubs. Be warned, if you get one as a present for your kids on a vacation to Ireland, they will insist on playing it *every* morning at 6 a.m.!

Ceilis

Few social events are as lively as a *ceili*. Imagine the lively sounds of jigs and reels wafting on the soft evening air from a cozy little village hall. As you got closer you'd hear the thundering of dozens of pairs of feet in syncopated rhythm. You'd know there must be a ceili tonight—and there are few better chances to see the Irish demonstrate their love of *craic* (page 120) and all-around craziness. Everybody alternates in dancing with everybody else of all ages, so you don't need to bring a partner. This means whether you're looking for a love interest or just some new friends, you won't be disappointed either way. There are approximately 30 ceili dances codified by the Irish Dancing Commission. They're all rather intricate—as well as excellent exercise. Dancers are certain to work up a sweat and a thirst! Most important for newcomers to this style of dancing, there's usually a teacher available to help even absolute beginners join in the madcap fun. But be warned, like most aspects of Irish culture, once you catch the ceili bug, there is no known cure.

Tin Whistle

Few instruments are more characteristic of traditional Irish music than the tin whistle. Its melody can range from chirpy and jaunty all the way to plaintive and haunting. Well-suited to the diverse range of Irish music, it is equally appropriate for cheery reels or slow, mournful laments. First widely manufactured in the mid-19th century, it became accessible on a large scale due both to its low cost (many were just a penny) and the relative ease of learning it. Although it is a straightforward instrument to learn, a range of simple techniques such as simply changing the airflow by use of the tongue or brief staccato movements off the finger holes can produce interesting ornamentation and impressive effects. While it is used in a number of different musical traditions, it should be no surprise to learn that the overwhelming majority of sheet music produced for the tin whistle is in the traditional Irish genre. Incredibly portable, this versatile little instrument became popular at Irish gatherings because it could easily fit in the inside breast pocket of a jacket. Whether you're passing an impromptu gathering of street musicians or participating in rollicking wedding celebrations, if you hear the tin whistle's distinctive tones, you're probably among a group of fellow Irish musical aficionados. So get jiggin'!

Uilleann Pipes

The uilleann pipes are Ireland's much-improved version 2.0 of the bagpipes. These Irish variants are notably superior to their Scottish cousin in many nifty ways. They're neat and compact and would probably fit inside the average grade-schooler's backpack. Using the elbow for the drone frees up the musician to sing, carry on a conversation, or drink a pint while playing. Try doing any of that while blowing into a set of Scottish pipes. (You can't play Scottish pipes sitting down; they're made to be played standing up.) Overall, for ease of use, portability, and all-around versatility, the uilleann pipes are the only way to go!

Harps and Heraldry

It's fitting that Ireland, a nation so celebrated for its musical accomplishments, is the only country in the world to have a musical instrument as its official symbol. Our traditional Irish harp—a symbol of Irish pride that we all know and love so well—was considered a difficult instrument to play. It was even said that anybody who started to learn after the age of seven would never master its incredible complexities. Old-style harp strings were made of metal, and it was an unwieldy and expensive instrument. Therefore, harp music would only be heard in the houses of great chieftains on special occasions. The presence of harp music indicated a gathering of importance and an honor to those who gathered to hear it. A harpist was the highest ranking of all traditional Irish musicians and he would be deferred to and handsomely paid for his musical endeavors. One of the most visible icons of Irish identity, harps appear not only on Irish coins, passports, and official documents, but also in many Irish crests and coats of arms. Interestingly, the tune of the "Star Spangled Banner" was seemingly composed by the great Turlough O'Carolan, a blind Irish harpist who died about 35 years before the American Revolution. Unfortunately, there was a sharp decline in harpistry due to the Penal Laws and the subsequent decline of the old Gaelic lords. Organizers of the harp festival in Belfast in 1792 sadly found only 12 harpists in the whole of Ireland. Fortunately, like so many elements of Irish culture, the harp has been enjoying a resurgence of interest in recent years.

CHAPTER 7

Ireland's Legacy of Learning and Knowledge

The Irish thirst for learning dates back to when our monks helped preserve Latin and Greek writings, as well as the English language itself, by copying manuscripts during the 5th through 8th centuries, a time when Ireland attained the proud name "Island of Saints and Scholars." In Ireland's secure monastic enclaves, vital troves of scholarship in sciences and literature were held safe for all of mankind while the rest of Europe tumbled into the Dark Ages. This love of knowledge led to many distinctively Irish intellectual accomplishments, but perhaps nowhere did the Irish excel more than in writing fiction, where the great tradition of Irish storytelling is combined with our love of language.

It's the Way We Tell 'Em

The delightful Irish way of telling a story is a complex and elaborate one, complete with wild exaggerations, a certain delight in improbable fantasy, and a heightened sense of drama. It's rarely a case of "just the facts ma'am." This is no mere coincidence. Children are encouraged to tell interesting stories and to show off. In fact, it's often the case that they must perform for visitors to the household. As an Irish child, it is not just enough to exist and be adorable—you'd better sing for your supper! This uniquely Irish approach to telling a tale has its deep roots in historic tradition. You didn't think we all just miraculously turned out like that, did you?

Bards

The pre-Christian Celtic peoples recorded no written histories; however, they did maintain a complex and detailed oral history committed entirely to memory and transmitted by bards and poets known as *fili*. The bardic system lasted until the mid-17th century in Ireland. Bardic training was a serious business. A description of life at a training school for bards survives in the *Memoirs of the Right Honourable the Marquis of Clanricarde*, written in 1641–43. It sounds somewhat like *Shark Tank* meets *The Apprentice,* AND it all had to rhyme! As the book describes, when students were intensely composing a poem, they "work'd it apart each by himself upon his own Bed, the whole next Day in the Dark, till at a certain Hour in the Night, Lights being brought in, they committed it to writing. Being afterwards dress'd and come together into a large Room, where the Masters waited, each Scholar gave in his Performance, which being corrected or approv'd of (according as it requir'd) either the same or fresh subjects were given for the next Day." Who knew that medieval Irish poets were the real precursors of everything from the *X Factor* to *Iron Chef*?

Seanachaí

This uniquely Irish figure, part storyteller and part historian, was largely responsible for continuing the poetic and bardic traditions into modern times. In Irish storytelling, layers of culture are piled on top of one another to create a rich tapestry, combining narrative elements from Celtic, Viking, Norman, and English traditions. A good storyteller knew hundreds of tales and could perform them with typical Irish gusto and eloquence. In this informal way, an ancient oral literary tradition continued into the early 20th century. In a way, the Irish *seanachai* anticipated the modern trend for standup comedy. Both are well-rehearsed, but each has an element of live surprise, offering the performer the ability to react to the audience, adding extra flourishes here and there when they seem receptive and the moment is just right.

St. Patrick's Reports and Ancient FAQs

Among the most intriguing early Irish works are two by St. Patrick. His *Confessio* is a succinct autobiography aiming to justify his activities to the church in Britain, sort of like a performance report for his bosses, if you like. His later update, the *Epistola*, takes the form of a letter condemning the raiding and slaving activities in Ireland by British king Coroticus. Both were written in Latin sometime in the 5th century and preserved in the *Book of Armagh*, which dates from around 812.

Irish monks wrote in Latin. As it was not their native tongue, they had to come to grips with this most structured and unforgiving of languages. An Irish scholar called Asper reworked a grammar by the Latin grammarian Donatus and adapted it for the Irish market. *Ars Asporii* (or *Latin Grammar version 2.0,* as some might call it!), used a question-and-answer format. This probably makes this ancient manuscript the first FAQ the world has ever known. Take that, Silicon Valley!

Nabbing the Nobel Prize

For a tiny speck in the Atlantic, Ireland has made an outsize contribution to world literature. It's a legacy we can all be proud of, one that would take many pages (or indeed a whole library of books) to recount in full. Four incredibly creative Irish writers have won the Nobel Prize for Literature: W. B. Yeats, George Bernard Shaw, Samuel Beckett, and Seamus

Heaney. Eloquent Ireland has won this highest accomplishment in literature as many times as France, a country more than eight times its size. Yet these astounding accomplishments are hardly surprising considering that the earliest recorded Irish writing dates from the 7th century and was produced by monks writing in both Latin and Early Irish at a time when in the rest of Europe, most written knowledge was lost due to the armed conflicts, looting, and burning that marked the Dark Ages. Yet, remote Ireland kept the light of learning burning brightly throughout this entire era.

James Joyce: Literary Genius or Smut Peddler?

A point of pride for Irish intellectuals worldwide, James Joyce is considered one of the most influential writers of all time. The author's groundbreaking novels, including *Ulysses* and

Finnegan's Wake, transformed English literature with their experimental, free-wheelin' prose. Today, Joyce is the subject of high-brow literary affairs sponsored by official bodies such as the Irish Tourist Board. But don't be fooled into thinking Joyce is just for literary snobs—no way! Joyce was as lewd a sonofabitch as you can find in a waterfront Irish bar! His more graphic passages pay homage to some kinky shit, including oral sex and other dirty pastimes (have we convinced you to pick up one of his books yet?!). In fact, Joyce was so nasty that his novels were BANNED across the world! "Slim Jim," as the lanky, glasses-wearing, somewhat-sex-obsessed wordsmith was known, didn't let that stop him. Like many Irishman with a taste for sins of the flesh, he got off the saintly isle for better times else-where. No doubt he is cracking a wry smile in his grave in Switzerland—the sly old hoor.

Brehon's Better Legal System

You've heard we Irish are a lawless lot. But that should be considered a compliment considering we earned this reputation breaking (and rebelling against!) laws that were imposed upon us by a bunch of English wankers over the course of several centuries. Prior to that, we had our own system of laws called the Brehon law, which said far more than just "keep your hands off my whiskey." Being an archaic system, it was at times ridiculously specific, dictating things such as old people were to be provided with one oatcake per day along with a ration of sour milk. Surprisingly, though, the Brehon law was also remarkably advanced. It offered a progressive way of life and justice more humane in many ways than the one brought in by the English. For example, capital punishment was not a legal option. The emphasis was on restitution and making good rather than on punitive measures. Ultimately, everybody was seen as equal before the law, including women, who retained remarkable autonomy from men upon marriage and had the right to practice any profession they chose. Furthermore, any man considered too lazy or indifferent to satisfy his wife sexually was subject to a fine. Fellas, you've been warned. A "traditional" Irish girl might well insist you perform in bed or pay up.

Murphy's Famous Failure-Proofing Law

You might have wondered if Murphy's Law originally referred to a failed Irish rebellion or a series of disappointing crop yields. You might even have thought it was coined by Mrs. Murphy after a series of botched attempts to find a "nice young girl" for her eldest son! However, the origins of Murphy's Law are actually far more recent than you might think—post-war America, in fact. In 1949 Irish-American Air

Force engineer Captain Edward A. Murphy, Jr., realized during an acceleration-tolerance experiment that all 16 sensors attached to the test subject's body had been installed back to front. With typical wry Irish humor, he declared, "If there are two or more ways to do something and one of those ways can result in a catastrophe, then someone will do it." His quip was first recorded in engineering literature as a warning to others. Before long, Murphy's Law had become a common warning in all walks of life to prepare for the worst and always err on the side of caution. Murphy's motto demonstrates yet another way that the Irish have expanded American vocabulary and ways of thinking.

CHAPTER 8

A Way with Words Like You Wouldn't Believe

We Irish are known for our creative use of language. Whether we're winning Nobel prizes for great works of literature or coming up with the most inventively dirty swears, our melodious accents can create some truly unique phrases. But while we do have conversational conviviality and verbal charm, watch out if you get on someone's wrong side. We are also known for incredible skill with stinging put-downs and acid-tongued remarks; it's another way we stick up for ourselves.

Taking You Down a Peg or Two

This tradition of creative barbs and criticism has a noble and ancient pedigree. In Gaelic Ireland, poets of the highest grade were equal in status to lords. Chieftains retained bards to sing their praises. These poets were treated with the utmost respect and rewarded handsomely. Hey, everybody needs a little publicity. But watch out—if the perks and money stopped flowing, their harsh words would make boils rise on the target's face. Reputations built over years might crumble in the blink of an eye or the few seconds it took to "give out" or mouth off about somebody.

Tight as a Duck's Arse Underwater

Coming as most Irish did from a background where hard times meant you stuck together for the sake of common survival, the harshest insults were reserved for those who were miserly, didn't help their fellow man, or put on airs once they made it good. Lack of generosity and hospitality were the worst sins of all. Nobody wanted to be branded with having "deep pockets but short arms," or, more colorfully, as so mean that "you wouldn't give anyone the steam off your piss."

"Who Are You When You're at Home?!"

"This Irish distaste for jumped-up people who forget where they come from is best exemplified in the phrase "losing the run of yourself." This alludes to a young horse who tries to gallop when he's not ready—with disastrous results for himself and all around. Another Irish proverb warns of the dangers of newfound wealth: "If you put a beggar on horseback, he'll ride to the gates of hell."

Killing You with Kindness

An interesting subcategory of the classic Irish put-down is the booby-trapped compliment. Sly and subtle, these might be hard to detect. Practice will train your ear. The speaker's tone and emphasis get the message across.

"Sure, if it makes *you* happy, I wouldn't mind what anybody else says." (And believe me, they'll have a great deal to say.)

"Oh, I'm *sure* you'll be the height of fashion." (Just like, I'm *sure* my stingy brother-in-law will repay the loan he owes me.)

"You're *just* fine the way you are!" (Well, you'd better think you are, as it's far too late to change now.)

It's How You Don't Say It

Sometimes the Irish use the phrase, "If you can't say anything good, then don't say anything at all," in a particularly devious way. They give unenthusiastic praise in one area, masking scorn in another. A few examples will get you used to the hidden meanings.

"She's a lovely girl." = "If you like that brassy, devious type."

"She has a pretty smile." = "But the rest of her would turn milk sour."

"He always has a kind word for everyone." = "He's too stupid to have any clue what they're saying about him."

"Oh, sure he had brains to burn." = "And look what a feckin' mess he made of his life."

"They're very kind to their poor 'aul mother." = "But the way those mean, greedy, backstabbing bastards treat everyone else makes them a disgrace to humanity."

"Sure it's very cozy in here, and isn't it only sensible not to be throwing your money around?" = "God, this run-down hovel is tiny. I'm sorry my daughter married you."

"Well, at least you won't spend every waking hour pulling weeds." = "God, what a miserable little garden—it's the size of a hen's backside."

Ár dTeanga Féin

...or "our own tongue," as native speakers call Irish Gaelic. Next to Latin, Irish Gaelic is the European language with the longest continual history. It's one of the few Celtic languages that survived the rise of Germanic and Latin tongues and their accompanying armies, including those English hooligans, of course! Today 30 percent of Ireland's population claims fluency in Irish, and about 5 percent use it as their everyday language. Recent years have seen the rise of Irish-language radio and TV stations. Our complex, musical tongue lends itself perfectly to poetry and figurative speech, in which we are unmatched.

In 1500, the majority of Ireland's inhabitants spoke Irish as their first language. The noble Anglo-Norman families spoke both English and Irish, but the common folk used just Irish. As the English plantations took hold and waves of English-speaking settlers crashed ashore, parents had to give in to the trend and encourage their children to speak English just to get ahead at home and abroad.

In schools, children wore a short stick around their necks. Every time they used a Gaelic word, the teacher cut a mark on the rod. At the end of the day, the teacher doled out a beating for every notch. When the young students returned home, their parents did the same. It must have broken the parents' hearts, but they had to survive the new social order—even if it meant losing their beloved culture. Still, the Irish language, songs, and stories lived on in remote places with less English interference, especially in the West. The language, like the Irish spirit, refused to be beaten. These remote districts would save the living language and ultimately bring it back in modern times.

Irish is now the official language of the Republic of Ireland. Learning it is mandatory for all Irish schoolchildren. Visitors soon notice that signposts are in both English and Irish. Growing interest among many Irish Americans has led to American colleges and universities proudly offering courses in the ancient and melodious mother tongue.

If you haven't already, be sure to give Irish a try. The following common phrases can help boost your IQ (Irishness quotient, that is!):

Conas atá tú? ("kunus ah-thaw thoo")—How are you?

Go raibh míle maith agat. ("guh row meela moh ugut")—Thank you very much.

Tá Fáilte romhat! ("taw fawilteh rowth")—You're welcome.

Cad as duit? ("kawd oss dit")—Where are you from?

Gabh mo leithscéal. ("gauw muh leshgale")—Excuse me.

Le do thoil. ("leh duh hull")—Please.

Slán agat go fóill. ("slawn ugut guh fowil")— Goodbye for now.

And the ever-popular *Póg mo thóin,* or kiss my ass!

Cute Hoors

Always clever with words, we Irish are adept at creating inventive phrases. Take, for example, the expression "cute hoor." Cute in this context has nothing to do with your comely features or fair physique. A cute hoor is somebody who knows all the tricks and sees around corners, foreseeing all the pitfalls and managing to surprise everyone by coming out ahead. Maybe it's all those obstacles the persistent Irish have had to confront under British rule! A cousin to the sly devil, a cute hoor can seem harmless enough. He doesn't make his slippery machinations too obvious at the outset. To do so might put you on your guard, and that would be the very last thing he would want. A cute hoor excels at seeing the exception to the rules— long before anybody else even knows there's a rulebook. His crimes are just so ingenious that even if you're the soul of upstanding moral righteousness, you can't help but admire his nerve. Trust the Irish to define such a canny and conniving rascal with that much precision and flair.

Eejits

We Irish are known for our inventive and original use of language. *Eejit* denotes a clueless but basically harmless fool. Often preceded by the modifier *feckin'*, the term eejit does not necessarily mean lacking in intelligence as an idiot might be. Nor are eejits necessarily as obnoxious as louts. An eejit is more someone who has lost his way, strayed from the path of common sense, done something stupid but not so outrageous as to be beyond redemption. Given the

right circumstances—especially after pub clos-
ing—we all are capable of "acting the eejit." So
whether with slight reprimand or affectionate
caution, don't take it too much to heart if an
Irish person calls you a "right feckin' eejit."
You're not a fool (well, maybe just a bit). But
with some good-natured cajoling and some cor-
rective action on your part (cop-on, as we Irish
would put it), you're well on your way back
into our good graces. Irish culture is known for
its flexibility and willingness to accommodate
eccentricity and minor bad behavior. At least
until the next time you start being an eejit
again...

Feck—the Friendly F-Bomb

Now it's well-known that we Irish are
renowned for our use of language. You know
what I mean—those sad songs full of lovely
metaphors, blessings full of kindly figures of
speech. However, the Irish love of language

isn't just confined to the light and bright. We also have a way with cursing. Our history of struggle and hardship means we've had a lot to cuss and complain about—as well as the need to set other people straight when they cross a certain line! So much so that we invented our own take on the F-word that's versatile enough to be used in just about any company, from the haughtiest civil servant to the much-respected parish priest. We're talking, of course, about the Irish invention *feck*. Just one letter, one tiny vowel sound separates it from that harsh Anglo-Saxon expletive. Feck packs almost all the power, but with few of the consequences. People might cast a reproachful frown at you for saying feck, but unlike the hardcore F-word, feck is milder and gentler. It shows you feel like cursing and giving someone a piece of your mind but that you can also keep your fiery side in check. It's the classic nuanced Irish solution that allows you to say what you mean and mean what you say. Feck is our version of speaking softly and carrying a big stick! With feck in your vocabulary, you'll be sure to get your point across in forthright Irish style.

Gobshite

We Irish don't take kindly to people who are full of their own self-importance, and Irish culture is renowned for its egalitarian and no-nonsense aspects. So it's hardly surprising that we have a whole host of terms to deflate an overactive ego. The slang word *gobshite* is perhaps the harshest of our expressions of derision. An unfortunate gobshite literally spews excrement as he speaks (gob = Irish for beak or mouth). Even his ma and da will recognize his deficiencies early on. They might even feel that it might have been better for him to have been swapped at birth. A sundry laughingstock to all, a gobshite is only befriended by a kindly saint (somewhat possible) or a cute hoor looking to take advantage of a gobshite's vanity (far more likely). Oily, unctuous politicians are often branded as gobshites, as are pushy and browbeating salespeople and those who inherit the family business and lord it over their fellow employees without realizing they are not merely lucky, but also extremely undeserving of their random good fortune in the lottery of birth.

Great Craic

Famed the world over as a lively, gregarious bunch, we Irish place a great deal of importance on good times and sociability. *Craic* or *crack* is widely used in Ireland to describe news, lively conversation, gossip, and socializing. The term "crack" originally comes from the Middle English *crak*, meaning loud conversation or bragging. The sense of gossip or the latest news entered the Irish vocabulary from Scots through Ulster at some point in the mid-20th century, when it was spelled as "craic." Nowadays, "craic" is widely understood to be a particularly Irish form of lively good times or a festive atmosphere. If the party is a night to remember, the expression "the craic was mighty" is often used. If the party was an Irish one, you can be sure this is an accurate description.

Paddywagon

Phrases with *paddy* in them usually denote a connection to Ireland or Irish people. A paddy-wagon was the vehicle (first horse-drawn and then later motorized) used by the American police to gather inebriates, troublemakers, or others that might bother the upstanding members of respectable society. So what is the association of the word "paddywagon" with us Irish? Well, that all depends on who's answering the question. Some contend that "paddy" refers to the large number of law-observing and righteous Irish members of the police force who did their very best to keep America's towns and cities decent, law-abiding places to live. Others, slanderous black-hearted villains by all accounts, reckon that the paddywagon's main function was to round up those Irish needed to be taken somewhere quiet to calm down and sleep off their drunken excesses. Of course, the truth might contain just a little bit of both versions. We'll let you be the judge.

Streetwise Slang from the Old Country

In case you think the only phrases the Irish brought to the New World were colleen and *Erin go Bragh* let's just set the record straight, shall we? Using "buns" to refer to a shapely rear end comes from the Gaelic geographic term *bunn* for base or lower part, as in the bottom of a hill. Then there's slogan. We're familiar with it nowadays from insipid political rallies and bland advertising campaigns. However, it's likely derived from the rousing *slua ghairm*, which means the yell of the crowd or a battle cry. Suddenly, all those phony catchphrases seem livelier, especially if you know that "phony" is said to come from *fáinne*, the Gaelic word for ring. Passing off brass trinkets as gold was one means for Irish immigrants who weren't experiencing too much of that famous Irish luck to earn money. Before we put the *kibosh* on all such tales of shameful shenanigans, I bet you didn't know that word comes from *caib a'bhais*, or the cap a magistrate would wear while handing down a death sentence. You dig? I'm sure you do, as dig in this context is a form of the Irish verb *tuig*, to understand.

Speaking of Brogues

Most readers are familiar with the use of *brogue* to mean a strong Irish accent, probably peppered with heaps of cute Irish expressions and witty turns of phrase. However, "brogue," or *bróg* as it's spelled in the original Gaelic, means shoe. This meaning lingers on in the term applied to those natty gents' shoes with punched-out swirly patterns. Yet, the mystery remains, why would a strong Irish accent be described as a shoe? Were those new arrivals from Ireland in the habit of wearing sturdy workmen's boots? Did they refer frequently and conspicuously to their shoes as brogues? Was this usage so common that it become synonymous with their style of speaking? There seems to have been a connection between what Irishmen wore on their feet and what came out of their mouths—and some would say we've been putting our feet in our mouths ever since!

They Said What?!

It seems everybody, Irish or not, has an opinion about the Irish, whether they're words of praise or derision. And who asked them, thank you very much? The following is a small but fascinating sample of what's been said down through the years. It's yet another proof that our tiny island nation has had a global impact unlike any other.

In order to find his equal, an Irishman is forced to talk to God.

> Character of Irish Stephen in the
> 1995 movie version of *Braveheart*

It's not that the Irish are cynical. It's rather that they have a wonderful lack of respect for everything and everybody.

> Brendan Behan (1923–64),
> Irish dramatist and author

We make out of the quarrel with others, rhetoric, but of the quarrel with ourselves, poetry.

> W. B. Yeats (1865–1939), Irish writer,
> dramatist, poet, and winner of the
> 1923 Nobel Prize for Literature

*Ah, Ireland... That damnable, delightful
country, where everything that is right is the
opposite of what it ought to be.*

>Benjamin Disraeli (1804–81),
>two-time British Prime Minster

*There are several sorts of power working at
the fabric of this Republic: waterpower, steam
power, horsepower, and Irish power.*

>*New York* newspaper, 1847

*A nation reveals itself not only by the men it
produces but also by the men it honors, the
men it remembers.*

>John Fitzgerald Kennedy
>(1917–63), US President

*There is an Irish way of paying compliments
as though they were irresistible truths,
which makes what would otherwise be an
impertinence delightful.*

>Katherine Tynan Hinkson
>(1859–1931), Irish-born writer

*My father was totally Irish, and so I went
to Ireland once. I found it to be very much*

like New York (state), for it was a beautiful country, and both the women and men were good-looking.

> James Cagney (1899–1996), Irish-American movie star and tough guy

If this humor be the safety of our race, then it is due largely to the infusion into the American people of the Irish brain.

> William Howard Taft (1857–1930), US President

When anyone asks me about the Irish character, I say look at the trees. Maimed, stark, and misshapen, but ferociously tenacious.

> Edna O'Brien (b. 1930), Irish writer

I showed my appreciation of my native land in the usual Irish way: by getting out of it as soon as I possibly could.

> George Bernard Shaw (1856–1950), Irish literary critic, playwright, and essayist, and winner of the 1925 Nobel Prize for Literature

For the great Gaels of Ireland
Are the men that God made mad,
For all their wars are merry,
And all their songs are sad.

> G. K. Chesterton (1874–1936),
> English-born critic, essayist,
> novelist, and poet

I was elected by the women of Ireland, who
instead of rocking the cradle, rocked the
system.

> Mary Robinson (b. 1944), first
> Irish female president

We have always found the Irish a bit odd. They
refuse to be English.

> Winston Churchill (1874–1965),
> British Prime Minister

Ninety percent I'll spend on good times,
women, and Irish whiskey. The other ten
percent I'll probably waste.

> George Best (1946–2005),
> Belfast-born soccer star

*You know it's summer in Ireland when the
rain gets warmer.*

> Hal Roach (1892–1992), film producer

*Ireland, thou friend of my country in my
country's most friendless days, much injured,
much enduring land, accept this poor tribute
from one who esteems thy worth, and mourns
thy desolation.*

> George Washington, speaking
> of Ireland's support for America
> during the revolution

*I had to have some balls to be Irish Catholic
in South London. Most of that time I spent
fighting.*

> Pierce Brosnan (b. 1953), Ireland-
> born actor who played James Bond

I'm Irish. I think about death all the time.

> Jack Nicholson (b. 1937),
> actor and director

CHAPTER 9

More Magic and Mystery Than You Could Shake a Stick At

We Irish may be no-bullshit, hardy people, but our culture is also steeped in magic and myths—and I don't mean the jolly leprechaun from the cereal box. Irish mythical creatures are nothing to mess with. From fantastical shape-shifting beings to screeching banshees and mischievous fairies, Irish folklore should not be underestimated. Otherwise, a curse with your name on it might just be conjured up.

The Blarney Stone

The Blarney Stone is a limestone block built into the battlements of Blarney Castle, about 5 miles from Cork City. According to legend, kissing the stone grants you great ability in flattering others. The most common story of the stone's powers comes from the 16th century Earl of Blarney. He gave such a convoluted speech when asked to declare his loyalty to Queen Elizabeth that nobody could tell whether it was tongue-in-cheek or true praise. In any case, it did the trick, and Elizabeth let him remain on his lands. We know the Blarney Stone works, of course, since none are better speakers, storytellers, or poets than us Irish. It's all down to the gift of gab—it's in our blood, in our bones, and *even* in our stones.

Tara's Throne and the Stone That Screamed

Forget that boring, silent, king-picking rock and that old sword Excalibur. Its Irish counterpart, not unlike the Irish themselves, is unafraid to make some noise! The Hill of Tara is an archaeological site in County Meath that contains a number of ancient monuments, and was, according to tradition, the seat of the High Kings of Ireland. In the middle of the main enclosure is a standing stone, which is believed to be the *Lia Fáil* (Stone of Destiny) at which coronation ceremonies for the High Kings took place. Legend has it that the stone would utter a scream that could be heard all over Ireland if touched by a true contender for Ireland's throne. Tara has played an important part in Irish history on subsequent occasions. As part of the 1798 rebellion, the United Irishmen set up camp on the hill but were eventually attacked and defeated by British troops. In 1843, Irish nationalist, politician, and famed orator Daniel O'Connell hosted a peaceful political demonstration here, attended by 750,000 people, that called for the repeal of the union with Great Britain. Archaeologists now believe that there may be several other undiscovered historical sites in the vicinity. As a result, plans to build a motorway nearby have been met with serious concern. The Hill of Tara was included in the World Monuments Fund's 2008 Watch List of the 100 Most Endangered Sites in the world.

Banshees

Bean sí in Gaelic simply means fairy woman. *Harmless enough,* you might think. But this fearsome creature isn't like any fairy princess you've seen in a theme park. This fairy doesn't just hover around, waiting for young women to come up with wishes. You see, the banshee's wail foretells certain death. Several Irish families even have their own personal messenger of mortality. You can't order that service online!

The banshee is heard more frequently than she is seen, which is a blessing. Her call is described as a blood-curdling shriek you're not likely to forget in a hurry. Those who catch a glimpse of her have even more horrific memories. She's a haggard old woman of indescribable ugliness, wearing long white shapeless garments while she combs her hair. Beware if this ghastly apparition stops grooming her tresses. She may throw her comb in your direction. If it happens to hit you, you're destined to meet your end. Not exactly the cuddly little sprite that you had in mind, eh? Maybe it's lucky Ireland has a thriving pharmaceutical industry to help stop those banshee-induced nightmares.

Changelings

Now we all know that Irish children are as adorable as can be. How else would they turn out to be such amazing Irish adults? However, a compelling tale explains the occasional Irish tot who acts like a holy little terror. We just blame it on the fairies! You see, those otherworldly imps have obviously whisked your lovely darling away to the spirit world while they've substituted one of their own little ogres in its place. Because of physical similarity, the swap might not at first be apparent. That is until your little Sean or Sheila turns from an earthly angel to a howling and screeching rascal that outdoes every other child for 50 miles around in sheer unruly horribleness, bad temper, and ingratitude. No actual incidences of these horrific trades have ever been verified outside of folktales. However, some Irish parents bewildered by their child's bad behavior will swear that their own little devil surely is a changeling! We've heard that a certain Lohan family of Irish roots have investigated the changeling phenomenon as the cause of their daughter Lindsay's troublesome behavior! But that could just be a silly rumor.

Dracula's Irish Blood

Dracula, written by Irish author Bram Stoker in Dublin in 1897, has gone on to become the most successful horror novel of all time. In recent years the text has garnered intense scholarly attention, with its pages providing unique insights into colonialism, sexuality, and the position of women in the 19th century. Although set in Transylvania, many aspects of the novel may spring from Stoker's family history and Irish mythology. It seems the author of *Dracula* grew up hearing his Sligo-raised mother tell horrific accounts of witnessing unconscious cholera victims struggling to escape accidental burial in mass graves—gruesome real-life tales of the undead. In addition, the novelist's portrayal of Dr. Van Helsing fits neatly with Stoker's own brother, a renowned Dublin physician with scientific interests that included the field of blood transfusion and the treatment of insanity. Romania, Dracula's fictional home, apparently has no tradition of vampires, while the fearsome Irish storytelling tradition contains at least two accounts of evil overlords who demanded the blood of their subjects and had to be buried with wooden objects through their hearts. Was the setting of *Dracula* in Eastern Europe an attempt by the author to add a hint of exotic excitement for his readers? Or, maybe, he felt it was better for his own peace of mind to place all those ghoulish goings-on at a safe remove from Ireland's lovely shores? While literary experts will continue to debate the fiendish aristocrat's true nationality, I'm sure we can safely say he had at least some Irish blood gushing through his veins.

Fionn McCool

Thousands of years before comic books were heard of, the Irish were ahead of the curve by having their very own superhero—who was far more gutsy and gung-ho than anyone else in the world! And his name—wait for it—was McCool (well it's spelled in various ways, but McCool has such a sexy ring to it!). Fionn didn't limit himself to the occasional spot of laidback crime-fighting and lamely jumping from one building to another. His magnificent deeds truly were the kind that legends are made of. The Isle of Man, located in the Irish Sea between England and Ireland, is reputed to be a piece of earth that tough-as-nails Fionn picked up to throw at a rival. In some stories, Fionn is described as being gigantic in stature. Not only an incomparable athlete, he wasn't too shabby in the brains department either. Brains *and* brawn—the combination every true Irishman aspires to! As a boy, Fionn accidentally burned his thumb while cooking the Salmon of Knowledge. Forever afterward, all he had to do was suck his thumb to have all the knowledge of the world at his disposal. So, parents, don't be too hard on those kids who continue sucking their thumbs after babyhood—they could be future Irish superheroes in the making! Fionn is the kind of character who inspired hundreds of fascinating traditional legends. One of the most interesting of these states that the great Gaelic hero is not actually dead at all, but lies slumbering in a cave where he waits to come galloping to noble Ireland's aid at the time of her greatest need. Good to know that when the going gets rough, you've got a mythical Irish giant on your side.

Fairies: Fairly Feckin' Dangerous

References to supernatural beings abound in Irish folklore, the most famous of all being the fairy folk. Now, when you think fairy, you probably picture a fluttering Tinker Bell or a sweet little girl's sparkly dress-up wings. But these Irish fairies were far from a kid's cute toy. To put it lightly, they could be assholes, and many a tragic hero from song and legend learned the hard way that you do not mess with the fairies. The prominence of the *Sidhe* (which means mound-dwellers in Gaelic) is believed to come from the preponderance of earthen mounds where Ireland's earliest inhabitants had been buried or that contained the remains of forts where they had once lived. Later Irish generations were wise enough to err on the side of caution when it came to things that go bump in the night. They were unwilling to refer to these previous peoples directly as the Sidhe as they believed that doing so might disturb the long-dead presences from their graves. Instead they referred to them euphemistically by praising them as "good neighbors or "the fair folk," later shortened to fairies. Yet the Irish remained cautious of this presence in their midst, taking various measures to protect themselves against potential fairy incursions. Food was left out for them, the first drops of milk were sprinkled on the floor for their refreshment, and, since the fair folk of Ireland presumably had the same good taste as their human counterparts, the walls would receive a dousing of the first batch of precious whiskey from a still. In addition, holy water and religious symbols were also believed to ward off the fairy presence. Solitary trees and bushes in the middle of fields were believed to be fairy gathering places and were consequently avoided, as were paths reputed to have been originally developed by the fairies' comings and goings.

Scarier Than Green-Tinted Beer?

No, we're not talking about the holiday on March 17, with its roving crowds of amateur drinkers hurling green-tinted beer on one another's shoes. The biggest holiday the Irish brought to America was Halloween. Derived from the ancient Celtic festival of Samhain, this mystical night was considered to be the time when the barriers between living and dead were at their lowest. Treats of food were originally offered to keep the spirits content so that they would continue on their journey back to the other dimension and not tangle with the living on their way out the astral door. The original Irish version of the holiday also had bands of children extorting treats in return for not playing tricks on their neighbors, a tradition that continues in the New World version of this holiday. One part of the holiday that did change was the iconic jack-o'-lantern. Originally, these spooky decorations were carved from turnips, which had the benefit of ubiquity but were a bitch and a half to carve. But, of course, in America, everything's got to be flashier and, well, plumper. Those Irish immigrants understood the value of tradition, but between the size, the soft flesh, the bright color, and the built-in hollow middle, they knew a vegetative upgrade when they saw it, and thus the modern jack-o'-lantern was born!

CHAPTER 10

Religion

Travelers to Ireland will immediately be struck by the abundance of religious imagery in Irish homes and public places. Lonely crossroads and busy streets alike may be graced by a lighted grotto of the Sacred Heart or the Virgin Mary. Daily conversation in the Irish language includes the greeting *Dia Dhuit* (may God be with you) and the response *Dia's Muire Dhuit* (may God and Mary be with you). Of course, Irish folklore is laced with elements of both Christianity and paganism. There's something about this land that makes its inhabitants other-worldly and more spiritual than elsewhere.

Patrick's Purgatory

If you've overindulged on St. Patrick's Day, you can always make the traditional summer pilgrimage to Lough Derg, known as Patrick's Purgatory. The devout took (and still take) a boat journey to an island in the middle of the lake, where St. Patrick once retreated to face his demons. There, three prayerful days are spent subsisting on one solitary daily meal of tea and a slice of toast. The first night everyone stays up until dawn. However, they do so praying the night away in church. If you start to nod off, the other faithful will (helpfully) nudge you awake as it's assumed you don't want to be a quitter. As the rousing Irish hymn puts it, "Hail glorious St. Patrick, dear saint of our isle…Dear Saint, may thy children resist to the death; May their strength be in meekness, in penance, and prayer."

Parishes and Townlands

The parish is the focus of all traditional Irish life, accompanying people through birth, first communion, confirmation, marriage, and, ultimately, seeing them on their way to the next world. Even in urban Irish-American communities, the parish occupies a vital role not only in religious life but also in terms of sports and entertainment, education, and social services, including being a referral network for jobs and accommodations. Then there's the craic and merrymaking—not to mention matchmaking—that takes place at parish fundraising events.

Further back in Ireland's history, townlands were smaller units within the parishes; think of them as the equivalent of city blocks. During the Penal Days when Catholics were not allowed to practice their religion under pain of death, houses within a townland would bravely take turns hosting secret masses in their homes.

Fearless Catholic priests, all with bounties on their heads, traveled covertly to tend to their far-flung flocks. These dedicated individuals would often perform the multiple functions of traveling schoolmasters, and legal advisor, as well as clergyman. Small wonder then that ties formed under such dire and dangerous circumstances remain tight to this very day—whether in Ireland or emigrant communities abroad, Irish parishioners remain loyal to their parishes in that fiercely tenacious Irish way.

Wakes and Funerals

The lines between the living and the dead are somewhat blurry in Ireland. We honor the living and the dead—especially our ancestors. Indeed we see the dead as part of society, and not separate from those still on this earth. As a result, the fascinating ceremonies that mark the departure from one life to another are similar to those for travelers setting off on a journey.

If the deceased had lived a long, productive life and died under normal circumstances, an Irish wake had all the trappings of a riotous goodbye tour. It was an occasion for much merriment, with food, drink, and music in abundance, along with games, stories, and jokes, some at the expense of the dearly departed. It was a proper send-off to a greater reward. Although modern wakes are more sedate, they are still chances for people to congregate, linger, and socialize. One of the most popular radio shows in rural Ireland is still the weekly broadcast of local death notices, complete with days and times of both funerals and wakes. Attendance by a large portion of the community is evidence of common solidarity, our joy in life, and the remembrance of our heritage.

Irish Monasteries

Medieval monasteries were multipurpose communities. Each one was like an independent town, with houses and businesses surrounding the church. The enterprises run by the monks included breweries and beehives, making life sweeter in every way possible! In addition, skilled craftsmen made an abundance of precious objects such as chalices, crucifixes, and jeweled book covers. Most importantly, these settlements provided protection from invaders and marauders—notably the Vikings and their 60-foot longboats. One of the key architectural elements was the round tower. These served as both lookout and refuge. When threatening outsiders were spotted, the monastery bell would be rung. Then farmers and monks alike would gather up their valuables and food supplies, barricading themselves inside the approximately five-story tower until the danger had passed. Monasteries were also the repository of learning, where knowledge was dispensed in schools and important documents were preserved and copied, much like a modern-day university. The volumes of information contained within the monastery walls encompassed everything from medicine to law and holy books. In fact, when most of Europe fell into barbarianism during the Dark Ages, Irish monasteries preserved a great store of invaluable knowledge. It's incredible to think that the 7th and 8th century Irish countryside was dotted with hundreds of these remarkable institutions.

Will the Real St. Patrick Stand Up?

Like any red-blooded person of Irish heritage, you probably have a fair amount of love—and a healthy degree of respect—for Ireland's world-famous patron saint. He's up there with Santa Claus and Uncle Sam in that array of popular figures we all love and know so well. Or maybe you just think you know him. There could be some facts that might surprise you... So sit down, take a deep breath, and have a medicinal glass (or three) of whiskey at the ready. What you're about to learn could rock the very foundations of your world.

First up, there's the whole question of St. Patrick's nationality. The revered personage came to Ireland from Wales. He may have been the son of a Roman administrator—we're not really sure. However, he certainly wasn't Irish. (Cue the loud organ chord!) Second, the Irish weren't too kind to dear old Paddy when he first reached their shores. He was brought to the Emerald Isle as a slave and was left tending livestock on a lonely mountainside. We're sure that in his lonely captivity, Patrick never thought he'd be celebrated by parades, statues, and street names by Irish people across the world.

Our Patrick eventually escaped his Irish captors. Yet, on his return to Britain he was tormented by dreams of the Irish begging him to come back and tell them about Christianity. His pretty awful treatment at the hands of the Irish notwithstanding, Patrick decided to come back. The man really was a saint—what can we tell you?! Your world in a shambles yet? All your preconceptions shattered? Wait, there's more…

We hate to break it to you that St. Patrick didn't rid Ireland of snakes, since there weren't any there to begin with. Perhaps they knew he was coming and decided not to bother slithering their way there in the first place. Shattered? In tears? Well there's one final shocker for you. Traditional pictures of Patrick show the holy man clad not in green, but in blue. That's right, decking him out in green probably only started in the 18th century as Irish national-ism grew. This was because green was the color Europeans associated with revolution and the springing forth of new social orders. At least the dapper saint kept up with fashion trends!

Don't Knock It!

Situated in the west of Ireland, this strangely named small town with a population of just under 600 is not (as you might think) the home of the "Knock Knock" joke. Yet, for a village of its size, Knock, County Mayo, has played a huge role in history. The name comes from *An Cnoc*, which is the Gaelic phrase for "The Hill." It was here on August 21, 1879, that the Virgin Mary, together with St. Joseph and John the Evangelist, supposedly appeared. This led to the village becoming one of the top three places of Catholic pilgrimage in Europe, alongside Lourdes and Fatima. Local people saw the apparition as a reward for the Irish holding onto their traditional religion, and a sign that although times were tough, they would eventually improve.

The Irish have a long tradition of sacred pilgrimages all the way from prehistory to the current day, a factor that has helped them weather the tribulations of harsh economic conditions and brutal colonial rule. An astounding 1.5 million faithful visit Knock annually. Pope John Paul II made an official visit to the shrine in its centennial year of 1979. Originally conceived purely as a transport hub to bring pilgrims to the shrine, Knock/Ireland West airport now runs regularly scheduled flights connecting all the west of Ireland with destinations across Europe. They even have seasonal charter flights to and from the US. Nothing short of miraculous for a village of its tiny size!

Around Waaay Longer Than the Pyramids—Ireland's Oldest Religious Monument

Newgrange, an imposing prehistoric monument in County Meath was built about 3200 BC, which makes it older than Stonehenge by an impressive 1,000 years and the Egyptian pyramids by 600 years. The structure dominates the landscape, comprising a majestic circular mound with an intricately crafted stone passageway and burial or ceremonial field chambers inside. It is speculated that the site had religious significance for its Neolithic Irish builders, presumably connected with the sun and the passing of the seasons. Newgrange is precisely aligned with the rising sun, whose light floods the central chamber within the mound on the winter solstice for almost 20 minutes. People come from all over the world to witness this wonder. In fact, there is a waiting list of 15 years to witness this singular event. After its initial use, Newgrange was sealed for several thousand years. It first began to be studied by archaeologists in the 17th century.

Dubbed "the great national monument of Ireland," this is one of the most important megalithic structures in Europe, or the world for that matter. Did we happen to mention that it's older than the pyramids?

CHAPTER 11

Irish Bad-Asses

As you can tell from the previous entries in this book, we Irish do not back down from a fight. We had to struggle for our place in the world and we don't cower in the face of adversity. From inventing new ways to protest to participating in brutally tough sports just for fun, we know how to take our lumps and return them if necessary.

Home of Boycotting

People have said that when you mess with an Irishman, you might as well take on the entire nation. Boy, did they ever get that one right! It's no secret that we stick together and don't take kindly to those who treat one of our own unfairly. We're not timid about conflicts. Nowhere is this more evident than with the origin of the term "boycott." In 1880, due to a very poor harvest, struggling tenants of Lord Erne in County Mayo asked for a much-needed rent break of 25 percent. The haughty and unsympathetic Lord Erne proposed a miserly 10 percent reduction. The indifferent lord ordered his local representative, a certain Captain Charles Boycott, to start immediately evicting tenants from their modest holdings, effectively making the hardworking farmers both homeless and without a livelihood. The local Irish Land League decided to put a halt to the dastardly plan. It was agreed that nobody would lease land from, do business with, or interact in any way with Captain Boycott. The postman even refused to deliver any letters to him. The community stood fast and not a single individual deviated from the boycott. Faced with the inability to gather harvests or work the land, Boycott organized a force of British loyalists to man the farms. A force of 1,000 soldiers and policemen was requisitioned to protect the boycott-breakers. The locals stuck with their plan of passive resistance. Not a blow was struck or a harsh gesture enacted—just a stony silence and complete lack of collaboration or compliance. The harvest was gathered by the outsiders—but at a cost greatly exceeding its value. An effective tool of non-violent resistance had been developed by the Irish villagers—one that would later be used by Gandhi and Nelson Mandela. The notorious Captain Boycott went down in history as the infamous bully who greatly underestimated the cussed stubbornness of the Irish!

Savvy Sailor and Sassy Lady

Strong Irish women have a reputation for not tolerating any challenges to their authority. Yet few have been as feisty as the 16th-century pirate queen Grace O' Malley. Daughter of a

ferocious seafaring lord who controlled shipping routes off the west of Ireland, Grace was
told as a young girl not to come onboard as
her long lovely hair would get tangled in the
rigging. She defiantly hacked off her teen-
age tresses with a knife and took to the seas
to extort and plunder. Later, after a stint on
dry land, she married a neighboring chieftain
because she fancied the look of his territory.
The man himself, not so much. So, after a year
of cohabitation, she dissolved the bonds of matrimony by hurling all his possessions from the
ramparts and proclaiming "I dismiss you." She
held on to his castle—we get the impression
that he didn't dare to ask for it back! In her
more mature years, she developed a reputation
for dallying with burly young cabin boys whose
vessels her forces had captured. To the victor
go the spoils! When her sons and half-brother
were taken captive by the English, she went
to London to broker their release with Queen
Elizabeth I. Good ole Liz was used to folks
doffing their caps in her presence, so she was

presumably stumped when Grace steadfastly refused to bow in her presence. Impressed by Grace's directness, Elizabeth set the lads free. The pirate queen promptly left the rarefied court, returning to resume her lucrative domin- ion over Ireland's seas.

The Aran Islanders

These remote settlements off the coast of Gal- way are some of the strongest surviving centers of old Irish culture and language. Although crumbling into the sea, the massive Dun Aen- gus fort on the largest island, Inishmore, is one of the most impressive ancient artifacts in Europe. You'll be awestruck by the fields, cleared of rocks, where the soil was created by laboriously hand-mixing sand, seaweed, and manure. The islanders are a hardy and a resourceful breed. Their powerful ancestors built every bit without machinery by hauling baskets on their backs, with the occasional help of a donkey.

Unless you've been hiding under a rock since the days of Fionn McCool (page 138), you've no doubt heard of Aran knitwear. Traditionally, people made these substantial sweaters from unscoured wool that retained the sheep's lanolin, making them water-resistant. How clever was that! These garments were cream colored, with decorative cable stitching running vertically, parallel to the seams. The seas around the Aran archipelago are notoriously rough and treacherous to sailors. Rescuers relied on the one-of-a-kind composition of the knitted patterns, rather than faces, to identify those who came to a watery end. These hefty sweaters are now popular with fashion aficionados across the world. They treasure them as wearable artifacts of Ireland's rich homecrafting history. The fashionistas are just catching on now, but we've been wearing them for centuries.

I'd Beat You Blindfolded

The most renowned US chess player in the 19th century was a remarkable Irish-American child prodigy. By the time he was a mere 10 years old, canny little Paul Morphy was challenging some of the best players in his hometown of New Orleans. By the age of 20 the savvy young lad was traveling internationally and daring each country's best players to take him on. He trounced all the best chess players of Europe—apart from one who refused to play him. Young Morphy even played blindfolded and won! Maybe he had the legendary Irish gift of second sight? Unfortunately, no professional chess scene existed in the 19th century, so Morphy eventually gave up chess in favor of practicing law, a profession he followed until his death in 1884. We're sure his clients thought he knew all the right moves.

A Fine Sporting Tradition

Irish mythology is dense with accounts of athletic feats by the likes of Cúchulainn (page 140) and Fionn McCool (page 138), so it's no wonder that the Irish have a long and distinguished sporting tradition that extends all the way up to the present day. Bet you didn't know that Ireland has had its own Olympics since the Bronze Age. The Tailteann Games, as they were known, were athletic contests held in honor of the deceased goddess Tailtiu, the god Lugh's foster mother. Although historically attested games were held from the 6th to the 12th century, it is claimed that the origins of the Tailteann Games go back to 632 BC, or even as far back as 1600 BC (versus 776 BC for the ancient Greek Olympics). A modern revival of the games has been held since 1924.

Hurling: Ireland's Fastest Moving (and Ancient) Sport

Some smart alecks (you know who you are!) might snigger at hurling's status as a national sport of Ireland, yet the only projectile component to this proud and fearsome sport is the hard, leather-covered cork ball known as a *sliothar*. Fast and furious, hurling is considered the world's fastest field sport. Don't blink during a match, as sliothars have been known to reach 93 mph in speed and 361 feet in distance. It's an intense athletic pursuit with lots of daring leaps in the air. Despite the use of the 4-foot wooden hurley to hit the ball, helmets and face guards were only made compulsory in 2010. Unlike the case with its much milder cousin, field hockey, hurleys can be wielded at any height or swung in any direction so you never know which way is safe to turn. This ancient warrior-like pastime is thought to have existed in Ireland for at least 2,000 years. The earliest written mention of the game is in 5th-century Brehon law texts. These establish the extent of compensation to be paid for hurling injuries. They also specify that the hurley should not be used to strike a blow—well, not off the playing field at least!

Kings of the Ring

Given the reputation of "the fighting Irish" it's no surprise that Irish Americans have been eminent in professional boxing since its earliest days. Famed fighters include John L. Sullivan (1858–1918), James John "Gentleman Jim" Corbett (1866–1933), Jack Dempsey (1895–1983), and Gene Tunney (1897–1978). So powerful was the Irish status in boxing in the first two decades of the 20th century that it became relatively common for non-Irish fighters to adopt Irish names in the belief that it would boost their following.

Celtic Champions

Another prominent group of strong athletes were the Irish Whales, who were at the pinnacle of weight-throwing events in the first two decades of the 20th century. At 6'3" and 194 pounds, Martin Sheridan was the most respected and popular. This five-time Olympic gold medalist, with a total of nine Olympic medals, was described as "one of the greatest figures that ever represented the US in international sport, as well as being one of the most popular who ever attained the championship honor."

CHAPTER 12

Sexy and Romantic Sons of Bitches

The Emerald Isle is known far and wide for the beauty of its charming lasses and the rugged sexiness of its strapping lads. It's hard to say how we got to be so damn attractive, but according to tradition, Irish women who are not pop stars or beauty queens can achieve exceptional sexiness by rolling naked in the dawn dew in the middle of an open field on May 1. Lads, mark your calendars and splurge on a pair of powerful binoculars. Daring to go bare is nothing new in our culture. In more recent times, nude sunbathing and swimming have become more popular in Ireland, though we recommend you do your research before stripping bare. Besides, those Irish breezes could have you breaking out in goosebumps in no time at all!

Lively Redheads

The Irish are often portrayed as having red hair, a trait associated with intense courage, a fiery temper, and fierce animalistic sexiness. So is the Emerald Isle mainly inhabited by russet-headed men and women, with anyone of another hair color immediately identifiable as an outsider? Hardly. Nonetheless, there is a reason that the Irish are associated with red hair. The general proportion of redheads worldwide is roughly 2 percent, with about 5 percent of Northern Europeans having auburn tresses. In Ireland it's approximately 10 percent. So we have twice as much incidence of red hair as the rest of Northern Europe. In 1995 the gene responsible for red hair was identified. This showed that about 40 percent of Irish people carry the blazing gene. So even Irish parents with non-red hair can have children with distinctively scarlet tresses. In traditionally large Irish families, it would be quite likely then that at least one of the children would be a flame-haired little imp. Could this be the reason for the incredibly strong association of red hair with Ireland and the Irish? Interestingly, scientists are in the early stages of investigating whether the gene that marks red hair can influence pain sensitivity, perception, and, of course, pleasure! The reports are inconclusive so far, but there seems to be a difference in how redheads and the rest of the population experience and perceive pain (and physical sensations in general)—this may be the reason for the association of red hair with temper and a forceful nature. It could also explain the claims of Irish redheads being a rollicking good romp in the hay.

That Creamy Irish Complexion

If you listen to any random assortment of traditional Irish ballads, they'll be jam-packed with references to milky-skinned lasses with fair golden tresses. Now, while Ireland has become more multicultural in recent years and there are a reasonable number of Irish people who can go to the beach and come home with something resembling a tan, there are a significant number who peel at the very sight of a sunbeam or instantly freckle once the temperature goes above 65. A people's complexion is usually an adaptation to the climatic conditions, and it should be no surprise that those who claim a gray, windy island as their ancestral home tend to look more like a whitewashed fencepost than anything resembling a vision of tanned loveliness. This natural pallor is generally enhanced by a tendency to spend the afternoons of a July beach vacation perched on a barstool, only braving the water after 6 p.m. wearing a long-sleeved T-shirt and voluminous baggy shorts—preferably in a shade of neon green that does not enhance a wan, chalky-white complexion. Nevertheless, beauty is in the (Irish) eye of the beholder, and if we can't tan, we'll just join some fellow Irish for a midnight dip in a local *loch*. There's nothing like a pale white Irish butt glimpsed by the light of the moon! By day we'll stock up on gallons of sunscreen with an SPF of 95. By the way, Ireland is home to Europe's largest zinc mine, and zinc oxide, as we know, is one of the classic ingredients in sunscreen. A coincidence, or just a case of God looking out for his own? We'll let you be the judge.

Alluring Colleens

Stunning and seductive ladies have played a large role in Irish history. During English rule, it was unwise for Irish people to recite poems or sing ballads extolling the glory of their country, so they often characterized Ireland as a beautiful lady adored by all, dubbed Roisin Dubh, the mysterious Black Rose. Patriotism and pretty lasses have always been joined in the Irish mind.

Ancient legends told of Deirdre of the Sorrows. Although the loveliest woman in Ireland—and that's saying something!—she was destined to lead a life of great sadness. Betrothed to aging King Conchobar, she falls for the young and handsome Naoise. The lovebirds flee the scene, but Naoise and his two brothers are hunted down and murdered. The mournful blood-soaked tale ends with dazzling Deirdre killing herself and falling into her lover's grave. Such sacrifice for love!

Female fascination certainly influenced the course of Irish politics. Patriot and rebel leader Robert Emmet risked his life and was eventually executed—all because he moved his hideaway to be close to his secret fiancée, the fetching Sarah Curran. Fortunately, nowadays many beautiful modern Irish women thrive untainted by tales of sadness and heartbreak. Ponder the wholesome, raven-haired appeal of songstress Andrea Corr, whose pale loveliness has set hearts racing both at home and overseas. Then there's Rosanna Davison, Ireland's own Miss World, the tanned blonde beauty who has graced the pages of *Playboy*.

Sex and the Irish

When it comes to connubial bliss, the Irish took the saying "good things come to those who wait" more seriously than most. Traditionally, the average age of marriage for the Irish was older than it was for other Europeans. Many delayed taking the big leap into matrimony, wanting first to secure sufficient funds to provide securely for their future family—an arduous task in a country racked by poverty. Large numbers of Irish did not marry at all, some for religious reasons, others, it has been said, due to a certain shyness regarding sexual matters. Yet that prudishness didn't mean the Irish avoided screwing around altogether. For example, Montgomery Street in Dublin was once the largest European red-light district, with over 1,600 prostitutes catering to those looking for a quick, matrimony-free fumble. An old Irish song called "Take Me up to the Monto" documents this era. Substitute whiskey for pot and apparently this part of Dublin had something of the freewheeling atmosphere of modern-day Amsterdam. Unfortunately, double standards aren't just a new phenomenon. So-called fallen women were often treated harshly by their family members and community. Recent investigations have revealed the massive extent of the dreadful institutions known as the Magdalene laundries, where up until recent decades unmarried Irish mothers were confined to toil as washerwomen, both financially and spiritually atoning for their supposedly sinful ways. The uptight nature of the Irish wasn't restricted to real-life sex either! Even fictional fornication could be fair game. Ireland was famed up until the '60s for its stringent censorship of books and films. All it took was for one person to recommend a book as being indecent or a threat to public morals and it was usually placed promptly on the list of prohibited publications. In spite of claims to the contrary, James Joyce's *Ulysses* was never banned in Ireland; its sexual frankness meant it was not widely distributed but it was not officially prohibited. Incidentally, *Playboy* magazine was not made legally available in Ireland until 1995.

CHAPTER 15

Hell of a History in the Homeland

Ireland's history is a complicated and challenging one. There is a whole host of incredible tales with heaps of sorrow, heartbreak, skullduggery, and treachery. It's full of fierce battles and stoic suffering. What follows is a very general overview. And yes, we know there's lots left out, but hopefully this will serve to point you in the right direction as you recall—or discover for the first time—the history that has made us who we are.

Prehistoric Times

circa 8000 BC Mesolithic hunter-gatherers migrate to Ireland.

circa 3500 BC The Neolithic peoples of the Boyne Valley build a complex of tombs, standing stones, and walls over several hundred years.

circa 500 BC Celtic influence in art, language, and culture begins to take hold in Ireland.

circa AD 100 Defensive ditches are built between rivals Ulster and Connacht.

circa AD 140 Ptolemy's *Geographia* gives the earliest known written reference to habitation in the area around Dublin.

circa AD 220 *The Annals of the Four Masters* tell us Cormac mac Airt is ruling as the High King of Ireland.

AD 431 The Pope sends Palladius as the first bishop "to the Irish believing in Christ."

AD 432 St. Patrick returns to Ireland.

AD 563 Irish monastic culture reaches its high point.

AD 795 The first Viking raids occur.

AD 852 The Vikings establish a permanent fortress in Dublin Bay.

AD 988 Dublin City is founded.

AD 1014 Over 200 years later, those frigging Vikings are still pulling their raid and pillage bullshit on Ireland, but victory by Brian Boru marks the beginning of the demise of Viking power.

1167 Dermot MacMurrough seeks support from Henry II of England to reclaim his kingship.

1171 Henry II of England basically tells Dermot to go fuck himself by landing at Waterford and declaring himself Lord of Ireland.

1297 The first representative Irish Parliament meets in Dublin.

1366 The Statutes of Kilkenny are passed to counteract the decline of Norman influence in Ireland.

1472 The King of England, showing a keen sense of the true needs and concerns of his Irish subjects, sends an exotic animal (most likely a giraffe) to Ireland.

1494 Sir Poynings, England's Lord Deputy in Ireland, passes a law that Irish Parliament can't pass laws without advance English approval, which is kind of a dick move, but not entirely unsurprising, given England's track record.

1542 The Irish Parliament passes the Crown of Ireland Act, which establishes that a

Kingdom of Ireland is to be ruled by Henry VIII and his successors.

1594 The Nine Years' War rages in Ulster as Hugh O'Neill and Red Hugh O'Donnell rebel against Elizabeth I's authority over Ulster.

1607 The Flight of the Earls (referring to the departure of the Gaelic aristocracy) signals the end of Gaelic rule in Ireland.

1609 Large-scale colonization of Ulster by Scottish Presbyterians begins.

1782 After agitation by the Irish Volunteers, the Parliament of Great Britain repeals Poynings' Law.

1798 One thousand French soldiers land at Kilcummin, County Mayo. A combined French-Irish force defeats a British force at Castlebar. The Republic of Connacht is pro-claimed at Castlebar. The first United Irish-men Rebellion takes place.

1800 The Kingdom of Ireland is annexed to (big hell-of-a surprise here, if you've been paying attention) Great Britain,' and the Irish Parliament is dissolved.

1803 Second United Irishmen Rebellion: Robert Emmet attempts to seize Dublin Castle.

1829 Catholic Emancipation allows Catholics to sit in Parliament.

1845 Great Famine: This is one part of Irish history you've almost certainly heard about, and it was just as screwed up and awful up as everyone says. A potato blight destroys two-thirds of Ireland's staple crop.

1867 Fenian Rising, a brave revolt, is put down with brutal reprisals.

1914 Government of Ireland Act passes, which offers Irish Home Rule. However, crappy luck strikes the Irish yet again, and it's postponed for the duration of the World War I, which is supposed to "be over by Christmas."

1916 Easter Rising: The Irish Republican Brotherhood seizes key government buildings in Dublin but rebels have to surrender after a week.

1919 The First Dáil (parliament) of the Irish Republic meets and issues a Declaration of Independence from the UK.

1919 Irish War of Independence begins.

1921 Northern Ireland is established. In December, the War of Independence ends with the signing of the Anglo-Irish Treaty and the creation of the Irish Free State.

1922–23 Irish Civil War between those in favor of and against the Anglo-Irish Treaty, which sacrifices Irish territorial claims to Northern Ireland.

1937 The Constitution of Ireland comes into force, replacing the Irish Free State with a new state called Éire or *Ireland*.

1969 British troops are deployed on the streets of Northern Ireland, marking the start of the Troubles.

1973 The Parliament of Northern Ireland is abolished.

1974 A power-sharing Northern Ireland executive takes office, but resigns shortly afterward.

1985 The governments of Ireland and the United Kingdom sign the Anglo-Irish Agreement.

1998 The Belfast Agreement is signed. As a result, the Northern Ireland Assembly is elected.

2008 The Taoiseach (Prime Minister) of Ireland Bertie Ahern retires under allegations of corruption.

2011 An ongoing financial crisis places significant strain on the coalition government, and it is dissolved.

CHAPTER 16

Gaelic Geography Lesson

Ireland is 189 miles from east to west and 302 miles from north to south, an area nearly the size of Maine. It is on the same latitude as Poland, but warm ocean currents keeps it more pleasant than you'd expect. And while locals like to complain that it rains "all the bloody time," in truth it varies between 150 and 225 days a year.

True to its rural heritage, over 80 percent of the land is used for agriculture, resulting in the lowest population density of any European nation. And if you want even more solitude, there are approximately 500 islands, only 64 of which are inhabited today.

A. Malin Head
B. Giant's Causeway
C. Achill Island
D. Benbulben
E. The Claddagh
F. The River Shannon
G. Newgrange
H. Dublin
I. Cliffs of Moher
J. The Rock of Cashel
K. Glendalough
L. MacGillycuddy's Reeks
M. Blarney Stone
N. Hook Lighthouse

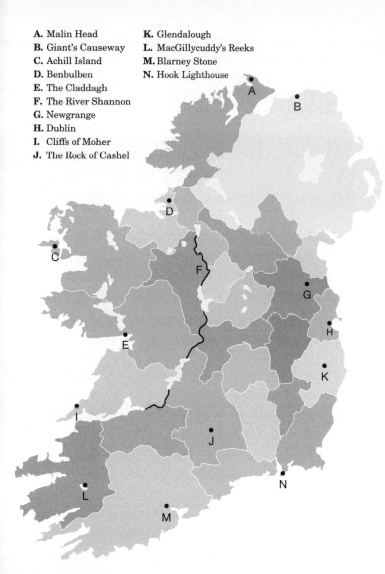

A. *Malin Head* (County Donegal). This northernmost point on the Irish mainland is the site of a weather station that closely monitors all those blustery squalls and rainclouds constantly coming in from the Atlantic.

B. *Giant's Causeway* (County Antrim). According to mythology these hexagonal columns are part of a passage built by Fionn McCool to challenge a Scottish giant to a fight. They met in the middle to battle it out, and the Scottish giant ultimately retreated, tearing up the roadway behind him as he went. Fact-obsessed scientists with no sense of romance would claim that the causeway is a volcanic formation.

C. *Achill Island* (County Mayo). Achill is the largest island off of Ireland's coast. Here you'll find miles-long white-sand beaches backed by cliffs and moorlands. Its waters are home to basking sharks, which are not dangerous—or so we're told. Your call if you want to skinny-dip under the moonlight.

D. *Benbulben* (County Sligo). Benbulben is said to be the burial place of legendary runaway lovers Diarmuid and Grainne, resting here together for all eternity. W. B. Yeats recounts how Grainne dumped Ireland's original super-hero Fionn McCool in his old age for the much younger Diarmuid. As ancient love triangles go, this one's a heartbreaker.

E. *The Claddagh* (County Galway). This fishing village in Galway Bay boasts dramatic sunsets and lots of fishing boats coming and going. If you feel like "putting a ring on it," we hear they've got some for sale.

F. *The River Shannon* (County Limerick). At 240 miles in length, the River Shannon is the longest river in both Ireland and Great Britain, entering the Atlantic Ocean outside the city of Limerick. Author Frank McCourt once said he'd like his ashes to be scattered on it "to pollute the river." Nevertheless, the wishes of internationally renowned Irish authors notwithstanding, it's actually one of the cleanest waterways in Europe.

G. *Newgrange* (County Meath). Dating from 3200 BC, this is the best-preserved passage grave in Europe. The monument's central room aligns with the rising sun on the winter solstice. Sorry, there's no use trying on Ticketmaster—this attraction is booked solid for the next 15 years, and they've closed the waiting list.

H. *Dublin* (County Dublin). The name of this fair city on the Liffey comes from Dubh Linn, Gaelic for "Black Pool." The Irish capital is legendary for the wit and sophistication of its citizens, including such notable examples as Oscar Wilde, George Bernard Shaw, and Jonathan Swift. And there is no shortage of places to meet its citizens as Dublin boasts an incredible number of pubs: supposedly one for every 100 people. Plus, of course, it's home to the original Guinness brewery.

I. *Cliffs of Moher* (County Clare). From Hag's Head in the south, these dramatic sea cliffs reach their full height of 702 feet just north of O'Brien's Tower. The views of the Aran Islands and the Twelve Bens Mountains of Connemara will take your breath away—and that's before you even look down!

J. *The Rock of Cashel* (County Tipperary). Seat of the kings of Munster and later donated to the church, this complex is home to some of Europe's finest Celtic stone carvings and medieval architecture. The rock is supposed to have landed here when St. Patrick was chasing Satan from a cave in nearby Devil's Bit. Nice throw, Paddy!

K. *Glendalough* (County Wicklow). This remote monastic settlement was founded by St. Kevin. It's nestled in an exceptionally picturesque glacial valley with two unspoiled lakes. Its inaccessible location allowed the monks to lead lives of prayer and contemplation. Once the tourist buses leave at night, it's still very peaceful—not a Jet Ski or concession stand in sight.

L. *MacGillycuddy's Reeks* (County Kerry). Apart from having a name that just trips off your tongue, this mountain range also has the highest mountain on the island, Carrantuohill (3,414 feet). The name refers to a family who were local landowners until the end of the 20th century. Bet your backyard doesn't look like this!

M. *Blarney Stone* (County Cork). Kissing it may give you the "gift of the gab." They'll even give you a certificate of eloquence to hang on your wall. Reaching the stone is pretty much guaranteed to give you a stiff neck. There are also certain hygienic considerations to bear in mind. Flu season, anyone?

N. *Hook Lighthouse* (County Wexford). This is thought to be the oldest working lighthouses in Europe, or possibly in the world. The current structure was completed in either the late-12th or early 13th century. The first lighthouse on the spot dates back to the 5th century. What James Joyce dubbed "the snotgreen sea" hasn't gotten any less congested in the meantime.

About the Author

Rashers Tierney is an itinerant lecturer and anthropologist of note, presenting seminars across North America on all things Irish. His earth-shattering PhD thesis on "Flatulence in *Finnegan's Wake*" has been hailed as the work that "blew apart" the clique-ish inner circle of Joycean scholarship. He is currently at work on a study entitled "Brogue mo thóin," a controversial volume on the connections between the ancient Irish craft of shoemaking and renowned Gaelic curses.

F*ck You, I'm Irish is respectfully dedicated to Mr. Tierney's Irish-born great-grandmother, "Granny Bridget," a champion Irish step dancer well into her ninth decade—as well as an accomplished amateur philatelist who assembled what many believe was the largest privately-held collection of green stamps in North America.